W9-CSO-451

Book

BASIC ENGLISH GRAMMAR

for English Language Learners

Howard Sargeant

Three Watson
Irvine, CA 92618-2767
Web site: www.sdlback.com

First published in the United States by Saddleback Educational Publishing, 3 Watson, Irvine,
CA 92618 by arrangement with Learners Publishing Pte Ltd, Singapore

ISBN-13: 978-1-59905-203-8
ISBN-10: 1-59905-203-2
eBook: 978-1-60291-107-9

Printed in the United States of America
11 10 09 08 9 8 7 6 5 4 3 2

Note to the Student from the Publisher

Grammar is a very old field of study. Did you know that the sentence was first divided into subject and verb by Plato, the famed philosopher from ancient Greece? That was about 2,400 years ago! Ever since then, students all over the world have found it worthwhile to study the structure of words and sentences. Why? Because skill in speaking and writing is the hallmark of all educated people.

Lesson by lesson, this book provides basic instruction in the eight parts of speech—nouns, pronouns, verbs, adjectives, adverbs, prepositions, conjunctions, and interjections—as well as the standard patterns of English sentences.

All students of English, be they native speakers or those who are studying English as a second language, will profit from the fundamental introduction and review of grammar provided by SADDLEBACK'S BASIC ENGLISH GRAMMAR 1 and 2. Helpful marginal notes throughout the books have been provided to reinforce existing skills and call attention to common problem areas.

We wish you every success in your pursuit of English proficiency.

What you'll find in this book

1 Nouns

There are two main types of nouns: **common nouns** and **proper nouns**.

Common Nouns

Words for people, places and things are called **common nouns**.

▶ These common nouns are words for **things**.

ruler	chair	hammer	bicycle	truth
pen	table	saw	ship	calculator
crayons	sofa	axe	truck	television
pencil	loyalty	drill	ferry	fridge
book	lamp	ladder	train	cooker
dictionary	carpet	lawnmower	bus	computer
courage	telephone	spade	laziness	printer

▶ These common nouns are words for **animals**. Notice that special names for **young animals** are included.

animal	its young		animal	its young
dog	puppy		fox	cub
cat	kitten		elephant	calf
cow	calf		kangaroo	joey
horse	foal		bear	cub
sheep	lamb		lion	cub
goat	kid		tiger	cub
frog	tadpole		whale	calf

▶ These common nouns are words for **places**.

bank	airport	school	post office
hotel	gas station	university	police station
library	park	office	restaurant
museum	farm	mosque	supermarket
mall	zoo	temple	stadium
theater	factory	shop	synagogue
hospital	nursery	gym	church

These common nouns are words for **people** who do certain things.

singer	manager	sailor	gardener
dancer	secretary	pilot	police officer
artist	teacher	driver	plumber
photographer	doctor	writer	farmer
magician	dentist	friend	clerk
athlete	lawyer	brother	technician

Proper Nouns

The names of particular people, places and things are **proper nouns**. They always **begin with a capital letter**.

These **people's names** are proper nouns.

Robin Hood	Florence Nightingale	Mom	Miss Park
Aladdin	Muhammad Ali	Dad	Mrs. Taylor
Frankenstein	George Washington	Granny	Mr. Young
Harry Potter	David Beckham	Grandad	Dr. Lee
Santa Claus	Julia Roberts	Uncle David	Professor Raj
Mahatma Gandhi	Nelson Mandela	Aunt Diana	Jose
Confucius	Alex Rodriguez	Ms. Hall	Yang Ming

The names of the **days of the week** and the **months of the year** are proper nouns.

days of the week	months	
Monday	January	July
Tuesday	February	August
Wednesday	March	September
Thursday	April	October
Friday	May	November
Saturday	June	December
Sunday		

AUGUST

Sunday		4	11	18	25
Monday		5	12	19	26
Tuesday		6	13	20	27
Wednesday		7	14	21	28
Thursday	1	8	15	22	29
Friday	2	9	16	23	30
Saturday	3	10	17	24	31

The names of **special days** and **celebrations** are also proper nouns.

New Year's Day	Veterans' Day
Mother's Day	Thanksgiving
Independence Day	Memorial Day
Valentine's Day	Halloween
Labor Day	Christmas
Ramadan	Yom Kippur

The names of **famous places**, **buildings** and **monuments** are proper nouns.

Big Ben	the Empire State Building
the Sphinx	the Taj Mahal
Graceland	the Eiffel Tower
the Grand Canyon	the Golden Gate Bridge
the Sydney Opera House	the Great Wall of China
Buckingham Palace	Chaco Canyon Pueblo
the Leaning Tower of Pisa	the Statue of Liberty

The names of **people who live in a particular country** are also proper nouns.

country	people	country	people
Afghanistan	Afghans	Samoa	Samoans
Australia	Australians	New Zealand	New Zealanders
Britain	the British	Pakistan	Pakistanis
China	the Chinese	the Philippines	Filipinos
France	the French	Russia	Russians
Germany	Germans	Nicaragua	Nicaraguans
India	Indians	South Africa	South Africans
Indonesia	Indonesians	Spain	Spaniards
Italy	Italians	Switzerland	the Swiss
Japan	the Japanese	Thailand	Thais
Korea	Koreans	USA	Americans
Malaysia	Malaysians	Vietnam	the Vietnamese

Exercise 1

Write each common noun under the correct heading.

theater	lion	father	brother
doctor	restaurant	builder	stove
elephant	kangaroo	museum	library

things	animals	places	people

Exercise 2

Underline the common nouns and circle the proper nouns in these sentences.

1. I told Uncle John about my accident.

2. Kim and Stephanie wore masks on Halloween.

3. The lawnmower is broken.

4. We're going to the movies tomorrow.

5. The lion is playing with one of its cubs.

6. My sister's favorite soccer player is David Beckham.

7. I'm watching a videotape about the Sahara Desert.

8. The tourists visited Rome and saw the Colosseum.

9. Does this bus go to the stadium?

10. We're reading a story about a boy called Harry Potter.

Exercise 3

Read the following passage containing common nouns and proper nouns. Put a C in the box after a common noun and a P in the box after a proper noun.

Mr. Peters ☐ lives in Maine ☐ in a big house ☐ by the sea ☐ . He has three cats ☐ and a dog ☐ . He likes to travel to different countries ☐ . Last Christmas ☐ , he went to Paris ☐ and saw the Eiffel Tower ☐ . He enjoyed eating French food ☐ in nice restaurants ☐ .

Singular Nouns

Nouns can be **singular** or **plural**.

When you are talking about just one thing or person, use a **singular noun**. For example:

a tent	a park	an idea
a taxi	a doctor	an oven
a house	a lady	an exercise

Plural Nouns

Use a **plural noun** when you are talking about two or more people, places or things.

▶ Just add **s** to make most nouns plural.

singular	plural		singular	plural
a computer	computers		a mountain	mountains
a chair	chairs		a river	rivers
a train	trains		an envelope	envelopes
a player	players		an insect	insects
a teacher	teachers		an oven	ovens
a taxi	taxis		an uncle	uncles

N o t e s

■ Words called **articles** or **determiners** are used to signal nouns.

a river	**an** armchair	**three** biscuits
a castle	**an** idea	**five** eggs

■ The article **an** is used before nouns that begin with the **vowels _a, e, i, o_** and **_u_**.

an artist	**an** eye	**an** insect
an oven	**an** umbrella	

■ The article **a** is used before nouns that begin with the other letters, called **consonants**. But some words don't follow these rules.

• _a uniform, a unit, a user:_ **a**, not **an**, is used because the vowel **u** in these words is pronounced like the word **you**;

• _an hour, an heir, an honor:_ **an**, not **a**, is used because the consonant **h** in these words is not pronounced.

Nouns that end in **s**, **ss**, **ch**, **sh** or **x**, are made plural by adding **es**.

singular	plural
bus	buses
glass	glasses
dress	dresses
branch	branches
church	churches
beach	beaches

singular	plural
sandwich	sandwiches
witch	witches
brush	brushes
flash	flashes
box	boxes
fox	foxes

Most nouns that end in **y** are made plural by changing the **y** to **i** and adding **es**.

singular	plural
baby	babies
family	families
story	stories
teddy	teddies
fairy	fairies
puppy	puppies
housefly	houseflies
library	libraries
city	cities
lily	lilies
party	parties
dictionary	dictionaries

Nouns that have a **vowel** before the **y** are made plural by simply adding **s** at the end.

singular	plural
key	keys
monkey	monkeys
donkey	donkeys
toy	toys
boy	boys
cowboy	cowboys

singular	plural
day	days
tray	trays
runway	runways
chimney	chimneys
trolley	trolleys
valley	valleys

Many nouns that end in **f** are made plural by changing the **f** to **v** and adding **es**.

singular	plural
half	halves
leaf	leaves
shelf	shelves
wolf	wolves
thief	thieves

But some nouns that end in **f** are made plural simply by adding **s**.

singular	plural
chief	chiefs
roof	roofs
handkerchief	handkerchiefs
cliff	cliffs
puff	puffs

Some nouns that end in **f** can be made plural in **two ways**.

singular	plural
scarf	scarf**s** *or* scar**ves**
hoof	hoof**s** *or* hoo**ves**
dwarf	dwarf**s** *or* dwar**ves**
wharf	wharf**s** *or* whar**ves**

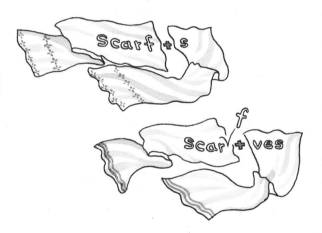

Most nouns that end in **fe** are made plural by changing the **f** to **v** and adding **s**.

singular	plural
knife	knives
wife	wives
life	lives
midwife	midwives

Most nouns that end in **o** are made plural by adding **s**.

singular	plural
video	video**s**
hippo	hippo**s**
zoo	zoo**s**
kangaroo	kangaroo**s**

But other nouns that end in **o** are made plural by adding **es**.

singular	plural
tomato	tomato**es**
potato	potato**es**
hero	hero**es**

Some nouns change spelling from the singular form to the plural.

singular	plural
man	men
woman	women
child	children
person	people
mouse	mice
tooth	teeth
foot	feet
goose	geese

N o t e s

What's the plural of the kind of **mouse** that you use with a computer? The plural is either **mice** or **mouses**.

The plural form of some nouns is the same as the singular form.

singular	plural
sheep	sheep (*not* sheeps)
deer	deer (*not* deers)
fish	fish (*not* fishes)
aircraft	aircraft (*not* aircrafts)
salmon	salmon (*not* salmons)

N o t e s

When you are talking about different kinds of **fish**, the plural can be **fishes**, for example:

the various fishes of the Indian Ocean

Some nouns are *always* plural.

trousers	glasses
shorts	spectacles
jeans	goggles
pants	scissors
tights	binoculars
pajamas	pliers

Some nouns are *usually* plural.

shoes	chopsticks
sandals	gloves
slippers	clogs
boots	socks

Notes

You can use **a pair of** with these plural nouns. For example:

a pair of trousers
a pair of pants
a pair of glasses
a pair of scissors
a pair of chopsticks
a pair of sandals
a pair of gloves

Exercise 4

*Underline all the nouns in the following sentences. Are they **common** or **proper nouns**? Put a checkmark ✓ in the correct box.*

	common nouns	proper nouns
1. Do you like cheese?		
2. They stood next to the Niagara Falls.		
3. May I borrow your umbrella?		
4. The ambulance was driving very fast.		
5. Carl did not agree with them.		
6. She loves to visit Disneyland.		
7. Would you like some more water?		
8. The fog was very thick.		
9. May I invite Tom to join us?		
10. My car is very old.		

Exercise 5

Read the following passage. Write S in the box after each singular noun and P in the box after each plural noun.

Our teacher ☐ is a very nice lady ☐ . She's very kind to all the children ☐ in the

class ☐ and she tells us very funny stories ☐ . Yesterday, she told a story ☐ about

the animals ☐ on a farm ☐ . They all had a race ☐ . The pigs ☐ and sheep ☐ ran

faster than the ducks ☐ and cows ☐ , but the heroes ☐ of the story ☐ were the

mice ☐ . They were faster than all the other animals ☐ , even though they had the

shortest legs ☐ !

Exercise 6

Read the following passage. Notice that the plural nouns are missing. Write the correct plural form of the singular nouns in parentheses. The first one has been done for you.

Three __ladies__ (**lady**) in pink _____ (**dress**) took their _____ (**baby**)

for a walk in the zoo. They saw four _____ (**giraffe**), three _____ (**hippo**),

two _____ (**kangaroo**) and an elephant. They walked for so long that their

_____ (**foot**) became sore, so they sat down on a bench for a rest near some

_____ (**monkey**). The _____ (**monkey**) were playing with cardboard

_____ (**box**) and throwing _____ (**stick**) at each other. After a while, the

_____ (**lady**) looked at their _____ (**watch**) and decided it was time to go

home.

Collective Nouns

Words for groups of people, animals or things are called **collective nouns**.

▶ Here are some collective nouns for **groups of people**.

a family	a crew
a team	a club
a community	a committee
a choir	a company
a band	a gang
an orchestra	the government
an audience	the army

▶ Collective nouns may be used with a **singular verb** or with a **plural verb**. If the group is acting as a single unit, use a singular verb. If group members are acting as individuals, use a plural verb. For example:

The crowd was orderly.

or

The crowd were clapping, yelling and cheering.

> **Notes**
>
> Always use a plural verb with the collective nouns, **people** and **the police**. For example:
>
> Those people **live** (*not* lives) in Asia.
> The police **have caught** (*not* has caught) the thief.

▶ Here are more collective nouns you can use for **groups of people**.

a **crowd** of shoppers	a **gang** of thieves
a **company** of actors	a **panel** of judges
a **class** of schoolchildren	a **platoon** of soldiers

▶ Many **groups of animals** have their own special collective nouns.

a **herd** of cattle	a **pack** of wolves	a **litter** of puppies
a **flock** of birds	a **pride** of lions	a **troop** of monkeys
a **drove** of sheep	a **pod** of dolphins	a **brood** of chickens
a **gaggle** of geese	a **school** of fish	a **swarm** of bees

▶ Some **groups of things** also have their own special collective nouns.

a **bunch** of bananas	a **deck** of cards
a **cluster** of grapes	a **flight** of steps
a **bunch** of flowers	a **suite** of rooms
a **bouquet** of flowers	a **suite** of furniture
a **range** of mountains	a **set** of tools
a **fleet** of ships	a **string** of beads
a **fleet** of vehicles	a **grove** of trees

▶ Some nouns name the **amount or form of something**.

a **loaf** of bread	a **bar** of soap
a **ball** of string	a **bar** of chocolate

▶ The words **a piece of** mean a single serving or part of something.

a **slice/piece** of bread	a **slice/piece** of cheese
a **piece/square** of chocolate	a **slice/piece** of cake
a **sheet/piece** of paper	a **piece** of chalk
a **piece** of information	a **piece** of advice

Exercise 7

*Read the following passage. Write the missing **collective nouns** in the blank spaces. Remember that sometimes there are two words you can use.*

Mom took Kate, Rudy and Derrick to the zoo. The zoo was very busy. A _____ of people had gathered round the monkeys. One of the monkeys had a _____ of bananas. Watching the monkey eat made the children feel hungry. Mom took a _____ of bread and some _____ of cheese out of the picnic hamper and everyone made sandwiches. After eating the sandwiches, the children had two _____ of chocolate each. Rudy wanted to give one piece to a monkey, but the zookeeper gave Rudy a very useful _____ of advice. "Monkeys may look friendly, but sometimes they are very fierce," he said.

Read the sentences. Does the collective noun indicate a group acting together as a single unit? If so, circle the singular verb. Does the collective noun indicate a group in which each member acts individually? Circle the plural noun.

1. The jury (were/was) arguing about the importance of evidence.

2. A whole company of soldiers (is/are) marching in the parade.

3. A gaggle of geese (is/are) running every which way in the barnyard.

4. Those people (live/lives) in North America.

5. The police (has/have) arrested the suspect.

6. That troupe of actors always (stay/stays) at the Grand Hotel.

7. The committee (is/are) handing in their ballots.

8. Our school band (play/plays) many lively marches.

9. A big colony of ants (lives/live) under the front porch.

10. The government (are/is) entitled to collect taxes.

Complete each phrase with a noun from the box that names a part or an amount of something.

bushel	scoop	ream	pair
drop	grain	pinch	galaxy

1. a _____ of stars   5. a _____ of potatoes

2. a _____ of sand   6. a _____ of bookends

3. a _____ of paper   7. a _____ of ice cream

4. a _____ of salt   8. a _____ of rain

Masculine and Feminine Nouns

Masculine nouns are words for men, boys and male animals.
Feminine nouns are words for women, girls and female animals.

masculine	feminine	masculine	feminine
boy	girl	nephew	niece
man	woman	king	queen
father	mother	prince	princess
son	daughter	emperor	empress
brother	sister	wizard	witch
husband	wife	actor	actress
grandfather	grandmother	policeman	policewoman
uncle	aunt	waiter	waitress

Many nouns are used for both males and females. They are called **common gender nouns**.

teacher	baby	doctor	scientist
pupil	parent	astronaut	president
child	cousin	dancer	manager

With animals, there is one general word for the animal and special words for the male and the female. Sometimes the word for the male animal is the same as the general word. Sometimes the word for the female animal is the same as the general word.

animal	masculine	feminine
rabbit	buck	doe
horse	stallion	mare
sheep	ram	ewe
pig	boar	sow
chicken	rooster	hen
duck	drake	duck
cattle	bull	cow
goose	gander	goose
fox	fox	vixen
tiger	tiger	tigress
lion	lion	lioness

Complete the crossword puzzle with the correct _masculine or feminine nouns_.

ACROSS

	masculine	feminine
3.	bull	_____
5.	man	_____
6.	fox	_____
9.	_____	princess
10.	_____	empress
12.	stallion	_____
13.	brother	_____
14.	king	_____
15.	_____	duck
16.	_____	witch

DOWN

	masculine	feminine
1.	_____	actress
2.	waiter	_____
4.	husband	_____
7.	nephew	_____
8.	_____	aunt
11.	_____	goose

The Possessive Form of Nouns

Use the possessive form of a noun to show ownership.

▶ To make the possessive form, put an **apostrophe** and an **s** `'s` after **a singular noun**.

> This is my bed and that is **Peter's** bed.
>
> We all like **Dad's** cooking.
>
> It is my job to collect **everybody's** plate after the meal.
>
> The flies are buzzing around the **horse's** tail.
>
> This is **Susan and Jenny's** room.
>
> This is **Tom's** hat and that is **Tom's father's** hat.

N o t e s

> ■ How do you make the possessive form when two names linked by **and** are the owners? Put an **'s** after the second name only. For example:
>
> **Katy and Mike's** house is very big. (= *the house that belongs to both Katy and Mike*)
>
> **Joe and Sarah's** dad works at the shoe factory. (= *He is Joe's dad and he is also Sarah's dad.*)
>
> ■ Sometimes two possessive forms with **'s** appear together, one after the other:
>
> This is **John's brother's** ball. (= *The ball belongs to John's brother.*)
>
> **Paul's teacher's** house has a swimming pool. (= *the house that belongs to Paul's teacher*)

▶ After **plural nouns** that don't end in **s**, use an **apostrophe** and an **s** `'s` to make the possessive form.

> The **children's** room is always messy.
>
> Some **people's** houses are bigger than ours.
>
> Rats' tails are longer than **mice's** tails.
>
> **Men's** voices are deeper than **women's** voices.

▶ After **plural nouns** that end in **s**, just add an apostrophe s' .

The **pupils'** desks are arranged in rows.

The **boys'** bedroom is bigger than the **girls'** bedroom.

The strong winds destroyed all the **farmers'** crops.

Mice's tails are shorter than **rats'** tails.

> ### Notes
>
> When a name ends in **s**, you can make the possessive form in either of two ways: add an apostrophe and an s 's , or add just an apostrophe ' . For example:
>
> This is **James's** house. or This is **James'** house.
> Which is **Charles's** bike? or Which is **Charles'** bike?

Exercise 11

Read the following passage. The possessive nouns are missing. Write the correct possessive form of the nouns in parentheses. The first one has been done for you.

Peter is spending the day at _____Tom's_____ (Tom) house. Peter likes Tom's family. He

especially likes _____ (Tom's mom) cooking! The boys play lots of games

together.

_____ (Tom) sister doesn't like _____ (Tom and Peter) games.

She is playing by herself. Sometimes the _____ (boys) games become so noisy

that Mom tells them to go and play in the garden. _____ (Tom) dog is in the

garden, lying in the sunshine. Tom wants to play with the dog, but Peter is afraid of the

_____ (dog) big teeth and sharp claws.

At 7 o'clock, _____ (Peter) dad arrives in his car to take Peter home. Tom says he

likes _____ (Peter's dad) new car. _____ (Peter) dad says that

he'll take Tom for a ride in it sometime.

2 Pronouns

A **pronoun** is a word that **takes the place of a noun.** There are different kinds of pronouns.

Personal Pronouns

Personal pronouns may be used as:

- the **subject** of a verb, or
- the **object** of a verb.

Subject Pronouns

The **subject** of a verb **does the action of the verb.** The personal pronouns **I, you, he, she, it, we** and **they** can all be used as the subject of a verb. Study the following two sentences:

> **Lisa** likes cats. **She** has four cats.

In the first sentence, the proper noun **Lisa** is the subject of the verb *likes*. In the second sentence, the pronoun **she** is the subject of the verb *has*.

Here are some more pairs of sentences that show **personal pronouns used as subjects** of verbs.

My name is Michael. I am fourteen.

My father works hard. He works in a factory.

My sister is older than me. She is twelve.

Our dog is very naughty. It likes to chase cats.

Bob, you are a bad dog!

David and I are playing football. We like sports.

Jim and Jeff are my brothers. They are older than I am.

▶ Object Pronouns

The **object** of a verb **receives the action of the verb**. The personal pronouns **me**, **you**, **him**, **her**, **it**, **us** and **them** can all be used as the object of a verb. Look at the following two sentences:

Lisa likes **cats**. She likes to stroke **them**.

In the first sentence, the noun **cats** is the object of the verb *likes*. In the second sentence, the pronoun **them** is the object of the verb *stroke*.

Here are some more pairs of sentences that show **personal pronouns used as objects** of verbs.

I'm doing my homework. Dad is helping **me**.

Goodbye, children! I'll call **you** later.

Where is John? I need to speak to **him**.

Miss Garcia is very nice. All the children like **her**.

The car is very dirty. Mom is cleaning **it**.

Uncle Harry called Mary to ask **her** a question.

My chocolates are all gone. Someone has eaten **them**.

First Person, Second Person and Third Person

In grammar, the person who is speaking is called the **first person**. The one spoken to is called the **second person**, and the one spoken about is called the **third person**.

Here is a table to help you remember which pronouns to use.

	subject	object
first person singular	I	me
second person singular	you	you
third person singular	he	him
	she	her
	it	it
first person plural	we	us
second person plural	you	you
third person plural	they	them

Reflexive Pronouns

Reflexive pronouns are words that refer to the noun or pronoun that is the subject of the verb. The words **myself**, **yourself**, **himself**, **herself**, **itself**, **ourselves**, **yourselves** and **themselves** are reflexive pronouns.

My brother built this computer **himself**.

Be careful not to cut **yourself** with that knife.

John was looking at **himself** in the mirror.

Kate fell and hurt **herself**.

Our cat washes **itself** after every meal.

We baked the cake by **ourselves**.

Come in, everybody, and find **yourselves** a seat.

The children cleaned their room all by **themselves**.

Bears like to rub **themselves** against a tree.

The bird washed **itself** by splashing in a puddle.

The players train every day to keep **themselves** fit.

Have **yourselves** a good time.

Here is a table to help you remember which **reflexive pronoun** to use with which personal pronoun.

singular personal pronoun	reflexive pronoun	plural personal pronoun	reflexive pronoun
I (subject pronoun)	myself	we (subject pronoun)	ourselves
me (object pronoun)	myself	us (object pronoun)	ourselves
you (subject/object pronoun)	yourself	you (subject/object pronoun)	yourselves
he (subject pronoun)	himself	they (subject pronoun)	themselves
him (object pronoun)	himself	them (object pronoun)	themselves
she (subject pronoun)	herself		
her (object pronoun)	herself		
it	itself		

Possessive Pronouns

Possessive **pronouns** are used to talk about things that belong to people. The words **mine**, **yours**, **his**, **hers**, **ours** and **theirs** are possessive pronouns.

This book is **mine**.

Have you lost **yours**, Tom?

This pen is **mine** and that one is **his**.

Sarah has lost her cat. Is this cat **hers**?

I can see our car, but where is **yours**?

We've had our lunch, but they haven't had **theirs**.

Here is a table to help you remember which possessive pronoun to use with which personal pronoun.

singular personal pronoun	possessive pronoun	plural personal pronoun	possessive pronoun
I, me	mine	we, us	ours
you	yours	you	yours
he, him	his	they, them	theirs
she, her	hers		

Demonstrative Pronouns

Demonstrative **pronouns** are used for pointing out things. The words **this**, **that**, **these** and **those** are demonstrative pronouns.

This is my desk.

This is the Mings' house.

That is my friend's house.

That's my mother's car.

You'll have to work harder than **this**.

We can do better than **that**.

It's raining again. **This** is awful!

Who is **that** knocking at the door?

Hi, Kathleen. **This** is Michael.

These are my pets.

These are sheep but **those** are goats.

Those are horses.

Notes

- Use **this** and **these** when you are talking about things near you.

- Use **that** and **those** when you are talking about things farther away.

Interrogative Pronouns

Interrogative pronouns are used to ask questions. The words **who**, **whose**, **what**, **which** and **whom** are interrogative pronouns.

Who used all my paper?

Who is Mom talking to?

Who are those people?

Whose pen is this?

Whose are these shoes?

What is your brother's name?

What does Tom want?

What is the date today?

What do you want to be when you grow up?

Which of these desks is yours?

Which do you prefer?

Which of your sisters is the tallest?

Whom did the President criticize?

N o t e s

- In writing and formal speaking, you can also use **whom** as the object of verbs and prepositions. For example:

    Whom did the president criticize?
    Whom is the principal talking to?
    or
    To **whom** is the principal talking?

    but you cannot use **whom** as the subject of a verb. So you cannot say:

    ✗ **Whom** came to the party last night?

    You have to say:

    ✔ **Who** came to the party last night?

- **Who** can be used as the subject or the object of a verb. For example:

    Who broke the window? *(as the subject)*
    Who are you inviting to your party? *(as the object)*

- **Who** can be used as the object of a preposition. For example:

    Who is Mom talking to?

- You can also use **whom** as the object of a preposition. For example:

    Whom is Mom talking to?

    If you put the preposition before the interrogative pronoun, you must use **whom**:

    To **whom** is Mom talking?

Indefinite Pronouns

An **indefinite pronoun** does not refer directly to any other word. Most indefinite pronouns express he idea of quantity.

Everybody is welcome at the meeting.

Many prefer their coffee with sugar.

Does **anybody** care for a cheese sandwich?

Few choose to live in the arid desert.

▶ **Indefinite Pronouns**

all	each	most	other
another	either	neither	several
any	everybody	nobody	some
anybody	everyone	none	somebody
anyone	few	no one	someone
both	many	one	such

▶ The pronoun **they** is considered an indefinite pronoun when it makes an indefinite reference.

They produce a lot of coal in your state.
Why don't **they** repair the bad roads?

Exercise 1

*Read the following passage. Write the missing **subject** and **object pronouns** in the blank spaces.*

My name is Charlie. _____ have two brothers. _____ are both older than

_____ . Sometimes they take me to the park and _____ play football

together. I like playing football with _____ because they are very good. We are

going to the park today. Would you like to come with _____ ? _____ can

all play together. Afterwards, _____ can come to my house if _____ want

to. I think _____ will like my dad. He is very funny and _____ makes great

pizzas. Do _____ like pizza?

*Some of the **reflexive pronouns** in the following sentences are used correctly, but some are not. Put a checkmark* ✓ *in the box if the reflexive pronoun is correct. Put an x* X *in the box if it is not correct. Then write the correct reflexive pronoun in the blank space.*

1. Sometimes I wash the dishes all by himself ☐ _____ .

2. Dad had an accident. He cut herself ☐ _____ with a knife.

3. Sally washes the car by herself ☐ _____ .

4. Do you think the doctor can cure itself ☐ _____ when he is ill?

5. The cat stays clean by licking itself ☐ _____ .

6. Anna and May made the dinner all by herself ☐ _____ .

7. Mom lets me walk to school by myself ☐ _____ .

8. Can you dress themselves ☐ _____ , boys and girls?

9. David can swim all by himself ☐ _____ now.

10. This light is automatic. It switches itself ☐ _____ on at night.

Exercise 3

*Write a short sentence using each of the **interrogative pronouns** below.*

Example: Who ___Who is this man?_____

Who _____

Whose _____

What _____

Which _____

Whom _____

30

Read the following passage. Write the missing **demonstrative pronouns** in the blank spaces.

Henry and I went for a walk on the beach. "What's _____ over there?" I asked. "It looks like broken glass," said Henry. He gave me a bag. "Put it in _____," he said. I put the broken glass into the bag. "We'd better put _____ in the trash," I said. He took the bag from me. "You have to hold it like _____," said Henry, "so that you don't cut your hand."

Exercise 5

Write the missing **possessive pronouns** in the blank spaces to complete the sentences.

1. I chose this seat first so it's _____ .

2. Can we borrow your coloring pens? We've lost _____ .

3. We live in the city and they live in the countryside. Our house is smaller than

   _____ .

4. John, is this pencil _____ ?

5. Sally is looking for her gloves. Are these gloves _____ ?

6. Can Julie use your bike? _____ is broken.

7. Tom got the books mixed up. He thought mine was _____ and his was

   _____ .

Exercise 6

Circle at least one indefinite pronoun in each sentence.

1. One never knows who might be listening.

2. Many are called but few are chosen.

3. I finished my cookie and asked for another.

4. Both were punished for the crime they commited.

5. Several applied for the job, but no one was hired.

3 Adjectives

Adjectives describe nouns and pronouns. They give you more information about people, places, and things.

Kinds of Adjectives

▶ Some adjectives tell about the **size of people or things**.

a **big** house	a **long** bridge	**tiny** feet
a **large** army	a **high** mountain	**big** hands
a **huge** ship	a **short** man	a **short** skirt
a **tall** building	a **thin** boy	**long** trousers

▶ Some adjectives tell about the **color of things**.

a **red** carpet	a **gray** suit	a **brown** bear
a **white** swan	an **orange** balloon	**green** peppers
a **blue** uniform	a **yellow** ribbon	**black** shoes

▶ Some adjectives tell what people or things are like by describing their **quality**.

a **beautiful** woman	a **young** soldier	a **flat** surface
a **handsome** boy	an **old** uncle	a **hot** drink
a **poor** family	a **kind** lady	a **cold** winter
a **rich** couple	a **familiar** voice	a **sunny** day
a **strange** place	a **deep** pool	**cool** weather

▶ Some adjectives tell **what things are made of.** They refer to substances.

a **plastic** folder	a **stone** wall	a **clay** pot
a **paper** bag	a **metal** box	a **glass** door
a **cotton** shirt	a **silk** dress	a **concrete** road
a **jade** ring	a **wooden** spoon	a **porcelain** vase

Some adjectives are made from proper nouns of **place**. These adjectives are called **adjectives of origin**.

a **Mexican** hat	a **British** police officer
the **French** flag	a **Filipino** dress
an **American** custom	**Washington** apples
a **Japanese** lady	a **Spanish** dance
an **Indian** temple	an **Italian** car

The Order of Adjectives

Sometimes several adjectives are used to describe a single noun or pronoun. When you use two or more adjectives, the usual order is: **size**, **quality**, **color**, **origin**, **substance**. For example:

a **small** **green** **plastic** box
     size   *color* *substance*

a **stylish** **red** **Italian** car
    quality *color* *origin*

Here are more examples.

a **large Indian** temple	a **tall white stone** building
a **colorful cotton** shirt	a **long Chinese silk** robe
delicious Spanish food	an **old graceful Japanese** lady
crunchy Australian apples	a **short handsome English** man

Adjectives of quality sometimes **come before** adjectives of size. For example:

beautiful long hair   **elegant short** hair

But adjectives of size **always come before** adjectives of color. For example:

beautiful long black hair   **elegant short red** hair

If you use any adjective of substance, it **comes after** the color adjective. For example:

a **beautiful long black silk** dress

Exercise 1

*Read the following passage and underline the adjectives. Write **S** above adjectives of **size**, **C** above adjectives of **color**, **Q** above adjectives of **quality** and **O** above adjectives of **origin**.*

Sydney is a large Australian city with busy streets and expensive shops. In summer, it's a very

hot place. People wear cool clothes and drink cool drinks. There are beautiful sandy beaches

where people can rest and look up at the wide blue sky. There are big parks for tourists to

visit. Japanese tourists like to sit and watch other people. British tourists take photographs of

the strange plants and colorful birds.

Exercise 2

The following passage contains a lot of adjectives. Some of the adjectives appear in the wrong order. First underline the wrongly ordered adjectives. Then write them in their correct order on the lines below the passage.

My friend Jeremy is a handsome tall boy. He always wears a white long T-shirt and a big red

cap. He carries a blue huge canvas bag to school. His favorite food is red crunchy apples

and he always has one in his bag. Our teacher is an English kind tall man called Mr. Clark.

He wears a blue smart suit and glasses with black plastic thick frames.

_____

_____

_____

_____

_____

_____

Adjective Endings

Adjectives have many different endings.

▶ Some adjectives end in **-ful**. These adjectives describe noun or pronouns that are **full of something** or **have a lot of something**.

a **beautiful** face	a **painful** injury	a **careful** student
a **cheerful** baby	a **joyful** smile	a **helpful** teacher
a **powerful** machine	a **wonderful** time	**playful** children
a **skillful** player	a **useful** book	**colorful** clothes

▶ Some adjectives end in **-ous**.

a **famous** writer	a **courageous** soldier
a **mountainous** area	an **adventurous** explorer
a **dangerous** job	a **poisonous** snake
a **humorous** film	a **generous** gift
mischievous children	**marvelous** results

▶ Some adjectives end in **-y**.

a **messy** room	a **noisy** car	**dirty** hands
a **sleepy** dog	a **cloudy** sky	**thirsty** children
a **muddy** path	a **sunny** day	**stormy** weather
an **easy** test	a **lazy** worker	**juicy** fruit

▶ Some adjectives end in **-less**. These adjectives describe a person or thing that **does not have something**.

a **cloudless** sky	a **meaningless** word
a **sleeveless** dress	a **fearless** fighter
a **careless** driver	**homeless** people
a **joyless** song	**seedless** grapes
a **useless** tool	**harmless** animals

▶ Some adjectives end in **-al**.

a **national** flag   **personal** possessions

musical instruments   a **traditional** costume

electrical goods   **magical** powers

a **coastal** town   **medical** equipment

▶ Here are some adjectives that end in **-ic**, **-ish**, **-ible**, **-able**, **-ive** and **-ly**.

a **fantastic** singer	a **terrible** mess	an **imaginative** story
an **energetic** dog	a **sensible** answer	**expensive** jewelery
basic grammar	**horrible** smells	**talkative** children
enthusiastic shouting	**visible** footprints	a **creative** artist
a **selfish** act	a **likeable** child	**friendly** teachers
foolish behavior	**comfortable** clothes	a **lovely** dress
stylish clothes	**valuable** advice	a **lively** cat
childish talk	**suitable** colors	an **elderly** man

▶ Many adjectives end in **-ing**.

loving parents	an **interesting** book
a **caring** nurse	a **disappointing** result
a **flashing** light	an **outstanding** swimmer
a **smiling** face	an **exciting** ride
a **boring** story	**chattering** monkeys
a **gleaming** car	**shocking** news

N o t e s

Words like **smiling**, **caring** and **flashing** are **present participles** of verbs. They are formed by **adding _ing_ to the verbs**. Many present participles can also be used as adjectives.

Many of adjectives end in **ed**.

a **closed** door	**satisfied** customers
boiled eggs	**worried** passengers
wasted time	**escaped** prisoners
a **painted** wall	**excited** students
reduced prices	**invited** guests

Describing What Something Is Made Of

Some nouns can be used like adjectives. For example, if you have a chair that is made of plastic, you can use the noun **plastic** as an adjective and say that the chair is a **plastic chair**. If you have a watch that is made of **gold**, you can say it is a **gold watch**.

But the nouns **wood** and **wool** can't be used like this. To make adjectives of these nouns you have to add **en**.

noun	adjective	example
wood	wood**en**	a **wooden** door
wool	wool**en**	a **woolen** jumper

Describing What Something Is Like

There's another way to make adjectives from nouns. Suppose you want to say that something is **like** a certain material, although not made of it. To make these adjectives, add **-en** to some nouns and **-y** to other nouns.

noun	adjective	example
gold	gold**en**	a **golden** sunrise (= *bright yellow like* **gold**)
silk	silk**y** *or* silk**en**	**silky** skin (= *as soft as* **silk**)
lead	lead**en**	a **leaden** sky (= *dark gray like the color of* **lead**)

Exercise 3

The following sentences contain adjectives made by adding endings to nouns. Write the noun that each adjective comes from on the line after each sentence. The first one has been done for you. Remember that some nouns must be changed slightly before the ending is added.

1. She's always making **careless** mistakes.   <u>care</u>

2. It was a very **painful** injury.   _____

3. Witches and wizards have **magical** powers.   _____

4. These oranges are very **juicy**.   _____

5. Dogs are usually more **energetic** than cats.   _____

6. Our neighbors are not very **friendly**.   _____

7. She keeps her toys in a large **wooden** box.   _____

8. Take off your **muddy** shoes before you come in.   _____

9. May I borrow your pencil sharpener? Mine is **useless**.   _____

10. What a **beautiful** dress!   _____

Exercise 4

Fill in the blank spaces with adjectives made from the verbs in parentheses. Remember that both present participles and past participles can be used as adjectives. Choose the adjective that suits the sentence best. The first one has been done for you.

1. It wasn't a very <u>interesting</u> (**interest**) movie.

2. We could hear the _____ (**excite**) fans screaming.

3. I hope the pupils don't think that my classes are _____ (**bore**).

4. My dad had a very _____ (**worry**) look on his face.

5. Have the police found the _____ (**steal**) car yet?

6. The supermarket sells lots of _____ (**freeze**) food.

7. The players on the _____ (**win**) team don't look tired at all.

8. Some of the old houses had _____ (**break**) windows.

The Comparison of Adjectives

The Comparative Form

To **compare two people or things**, use the **comparative form** of an adjective. The comparative form is usually made by adding **er** to the adjective.

adjective	comparative form		adjective	comparative form
dark	dark**er**		hard	hard**er**
light	light**er**		warm	warm**er**
high	high**er**		cold	cold**er**
low	low**er**		fast	fast**er**
old	old**er**		slow	slow**er**
young	young**er**			
rich	rich**er**			
poor	poor**er**			
tall	tall**er**			
small	small**er**			
soft	soft**er**			

Notes

The word **than** is often used to compare two things or people. For example, you say:

Mr. Lee is **taller than** Philip.

A car is **faster than** a bike.

The Superlative Form

When you **compare three or more people or things**, use the **superlative form** of an adjective. The superlative form is usually made by adding **est** to the adjective.

adjective	superlative form		adjective	superlative form
dark	dark**est**		warm	warm**est**
light	light**est**		cold	cold**est**
high	high**est**		fast	fast**est**
low	low**est**		slow	slow**est**
old	old**est**			
young	young**est**			
rich	rich**est**			
poor	poor**est**			
tall	tall**est**			
small	small**est**			
soft	soft**est**			
hard	hard**est**			

Notes

The word **the** is often used before the superlative form. For example:

A bee is a small insect. A ladybird is smaller, but an ant is **the smallest**.

If the adjective ends in **e**, add **r** to form the comparative and **st** to form the superlative.

adjective	comparative	superlative
nice	nicer	nicest
close	closer	closest
large	larger	largest
rude	ruder	rudest
safe	safer	safest
wide	wider	widest

Suppose the adjective is a short word that ends in a consonant and has a single vowel in the middle. Just **double the consonant** and add **er** to make the comparative and **est** to make the superlative.

adjective	comparative	superlative
sad	sadder	saddest
wet	wetter	wettest
slim	slimmer	slimmest
thin	thinner	thinnest
big	bigger	biggest

Suppose the adjective has two syllables and ends in **y**. Just **change the y to i** and add **er** to make the comparative and add **est** to make the superlative.

adjective	comparative	superlative	adjective	comparative	superlative
easy	easier	easiest	heavy	heavier	heaviest
funny	funnier	funniest	lovely	lovelier	loveliest
dirty	dirtier	dirtiest	pretty	prettier	prettiest
noisy	noisier	noisiest	tidy	tidier	tidiest
happy	happier	happiest	friendly	friendlier	friendliest
naughty	naughtier	naughtiest	tiny	tinier	tiniest

Use **more** and **most** to compare most other two-syllable adjectives. You will also use **more** and **most** with all adjectives that have *more* than two syllables.

adjective	comparative	superlative
famous	more famous	most famous
precious	more precious	most precious
handsome	more handsome	most handsome
exciting	more exciting	most exciting
beautiful	more beautiful	most beautiful
expensive	more expensive	most expensive
comfortable	more comfortable	most comfortable
delicious	more delicious	most delicious
interesting	more interesting	most interesting
difficult	more difficult	most difficult

Irregular Comparative and Superlative Forms

A few adjectives don't form their comparative and superlative forms in any of the usual ways. The comparative and superlative forms of these adjectives are different words, called irregular forms.

adjective	comparative	superlative
good	better	best
bad	worse	worst
little	less	least
many	more	most
far	farther *or* further	farthest *or* furthest

For example:

My painting is **good**, Melanie's painting is **better**, but Andrew's painting is the **best**.

Adjective Phrases

Phrases can be used like single adjectives to describe nouns and pronouns. Phrases that are used in this way are called **adjective phrases**.

Most adjective phrases come **after the word** they describe. Look at these examples. The adjective phrases are in bold and the nouns they describe are in color.

> Who is the girl **with long hair**?
>
> My friend lives in the house **across the street**.
>
> Mrs. Morris is **tall and slim**.
>
> This is the road **to Toledo**.
>
> The lady **in the bookshop** is a friend of mine.

Some adjective phrases come **before the word** they describe. The words in these phrases are often joined with hyphens.

a **long-legged** bird	an **eight-year-old** child
a **well-dressed** lady	a **ten-cent** coin
a **fun-loving** teenager	a **twenty-story** building
user-friendly equipment	a **large-sized** shirt

Exercise 5

*Read the following passage. Write the correct **comparative** and **superlative forms** of the adjectives in parentheses in the blank spaces. The first one has been done for you.*

Paul likes playing football. He's a very good player, but his friend Sally is a ____better____

(**good**) player. She's the _____ (**good**) player in the whole school. She is

_____ (**fast**) and _____ (**strong**) than all the boys, even the

boys who are _____ (**old**) and _____ (**big**) than her. That's why

Paul likes her. Paul thinks all games are exciting, but football is the _____

(**exciting**) game and it's _____ (**noisy**) than all the other games he plays with

his friends. When the grass is wet, everyone gets dirty when they play football. But Sally gets

_____ (**dirty**) and _____ (**wet**) than everyone else.

Exercise 6

*Complete the following sentences. Write an **adjective phrase** that includes the preposition in parentheses. The first one has been done for you.*

1. Is this the train __to Tokyo_____ (to)?

2. They live in a big house _____ (near).

3. Emilly's desk is _____ (oppposite).

4. The bucket has a hole _____ (in).

5. Who is the man _____ (with)?

Exercise 7

*Complete the following sentences. Write an **adjective phrase**, using the adjective in parentheses and another adjective linked with **and** or **but**. The first one has been done for you.*

1. My dog is __small and brown_____ (small).

2. His sister's hair is _____ (black).

3. Our teacher is _____ (oppposite).

4. Tomorrow's weather will be _____ (sunny).

5. The museum was _____ (quiet).

4 Determiners

Determiners, or noun signals, are special adjectives used **before nouns**.

There are different kinds of determiners.

The Articles

The words **a**, **an** and **the** are called the **articles**.

> The words **a** and **an** are **indefinite articles**. They are used with singular nouns. Use **a** before nouns that begin with a **consonant**. Use **an** before nouns that begin with a **vowel**.

John is reading **a book**.

Would you like **a peach**?

Is that **a dog** or **a fox**?

You'll need **a ruler** and **a pencil**.

Is there also **an entrance** at the back of the building?

Have you ever seen **an elephant**?

I always take **an apple** to school.

Do you have **an umbrella** that I can borrow?

Would you like to live on **an island**?

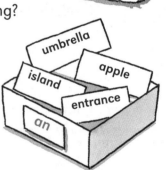

N o t e s

- **Some vowels have a consonant sound as well as a vowel sound.** Use the article **a** with nouns that begin with these vowels:

  Is there **a university** in your town?
  Does every child in the school wear **a uniform**?
  We are taking **a European** vacation this summer.

- Some words begin with a silent **h**. Use **an** with nouns that begin with a **silent h**:

  We've been waiting here for **an hour**.
  Meeting the president was **an honor** for all of us.

The word **the** is called the **definite article**. Use **the** before a noun when you are talking to someone who already knows which person or thing you mean.

Dad is sitting in **the garden**.

Who made **the mess** on **the carpet**?

Turn **the television** off now.

I'll wait for you in **the car**.

The boys are upstairs and **the girls** are outside in **the street**.

Using Nouns without Articles

When you are talking about something in general, not a particular thing, use a noun **without an article**. You can use **plural nouns** without an article.

Frogs are my favorite animals.

Children like playing games.

Babies cry a lot.

Glasses are things that you wear to correct your eyesight.

Birds are animals that can fly.

People enjoy watching television.

Nouns that don't show quantity are normally used without **a** or **an**. The article **the**, however, may be used with nouns that don't show quantity.

I like **sunshine**.

I sometimes have **fruit** for breakfast.

You've got **dirt** on your face.

A clock measures **time**.

Put **sugar** in your tea to make it sweet.

I need **time** to think of a new plan.

Would you pass me **the salt**, please?

Can I borrow **the paint** when you've finished?

> ### N o t e s
>
> You often use the singular nouns **school, home, work, church** without an article:
>
> We go to **school** by bus.
>
> Dad has already left **home** for **work**.
>
> They go to **church** on Sundays.

Demonstrative Determiners

The words **this**, **that**, **these** and **those** are also special pronouns called determiners. They are used to point out which thing or person you mean. They are called **demonstrative determiners**.

▸ Use **this** and **these** to talk about things and people that are **near** you.

Use **this** with singular nouns	Use **these** with plural nouns
Who lives in **this house**?	**These trousers** are too short.
This car belongs to my mom.	I don't like **these comics**.
Does **this key** fit the lock?	**These biscuits** don't taste very good.
This book is my favorite.	I bought **these apples** for lunch.
Who gave you **this money**?	Is there an adult with **these children**?
This cheese tastes funny.	

▸ Use **that** and **those** to talk about things that are **further away** from you.

Use **that** with singular nouns	Use **those** with plural nouns
This chair is mine and **that chair** is yours.	I gave my sandwiches to **those boys**.
That animal is making a funny noise.	**Those children** go to a different school.
Would you pass me **that book**, please?	These shoes are mine and **those shoes** are yours.
Who is **that man** talking to Dad?	These apples look fresh but **those apples** look rotten.
How much is **that dress**?	**Those people** are from Africa.

Quantifying Determiners

Words such as **many**, **much** and **several** tell about quantity without giving an exact number. They are called **quantifying determiners**.

▶ Some quantifying determiners are used only **with plural nouns**. They are **few**, **a few**, **fewer**, **many**, **several** and **both**.

Few people have been to the moon.　　We went to Europe **many** years ago.

A few children are absent today.　　**Several** friends went with me.

I have **fewer** CDs than you.　　**Both** brothers have dark hair.

▶ Some quantifying determiners can be used **with plural nouns and nouns that show no exact number.** They are **all, half, some, enough, a lot of, lots of, more, most, other** and **plenty of**.

All children like chocolate.
We've eaten **all** the food in the refrigerator.

Half the balloons have burst already.
Jenny spends **half** her time watching television.

Some girls like to play football.
Can I have **some** water?

Do you have **enough** books to read?
I don't have **enough** material to make a dress.

A lot of people like burgers.
There's **a lot of** fruit in the bowl.

They went to a park with **lots of** animals in it.
You will gain weight if you eat **lots of** ice cream.

You've got **more** brothers than I have.
There's **more** space in my room than yours.

Most teachers enjoy teaching.
Most lemonade contains sugar.

He likes playing with **other** children.
They had never tasted **other** food.

Plenty of my friends have seen the Harry Potter movies.
Drink **plenty of** water everyday.

Some determiners can be used only **with nouns of no exact number**. They are **little** (*meaning* not much), **a little** (*meaning* some), **much** and **less**.

> We have **little** time to play.
>
> There's **a little** rice left.
>
> Does the teacher give you **much** homework?
>
> I've got **less** ice cream than you.

Some quantifying determiners can only be used **with singular nouns**. They are **another**, **every** and **each**.

> I need **another** pencil.
>
> He likes **every** child in the class.
>
> **Each** house is painted a different color.

The quantifying determiners **either** and **neither** refer to **two people or things**.

> I don't like **either** drink.
>
> **Neither** sister has long hair.

Some quantifying determiners are used **with singular, plural or nouns of no exact quantity**. They are **any, no, no other** and **the other**.

> **Any** dog will bite if it's afraid.
> Are there **any** good books in the library?
> There wasn't **any** space in the cupboard.
>
> **No** child likes getting hurt.
> There were **no** pencils in the drawer.
> We've done **no** work today.
>
> There is **no other** way of solving the problem.
> She has **no other** friends.
> We have **no other** food in the refrigerator.
>
> Do you like this picture or **the other** picture?
> **The other** boys laughed at him.
> I like **the other** music better.

Interrogative Determiners

The words **what**, **which** and **whose** are used before nouns to ask questions. **Interrogative determiners** appear just before nouns.

>**What** time is it?

>**Which** boy is your brother?

>**Whose** pen is this?

Possessive Determiners

The words **my, your, his, her, its, our** and **their** are used before nouns to show ownership. They are called **possessive determiners**.

>I gave **my** sandwich to John.

>Is this **your** desk?

>Alan crashed **his** bike into a wall.

>Mrs. Park keeps **her** house very clean.

>The dog was licking **its** paws.

>There's a snake in **our** garden.

>Susan and Peter have invited me to **their** party.

> **N o t e s**
>
> The possessive determiner **your** can be used when you are talking to one person or more than one person:
>
> I'm very angry with you, John. **Your** behavior has been very bad today.
>
> Jake and Josh, **your** dinner is ready.

This table will help you remember how to use possessive determiners.

singular personal pronoun	possessive determiner	plural personal pronoun	possessive determiner
I (subject pronoun)	my	we (subject pronoun)	our
me (object pronoun)	my	us (object pronoun)	our
you (subject/object pronoun)	your	you (subject/object pronoun)	your
he (subject pronoun)	his	they (subject pronoun)	their
him (object pronoun)	his	them (object pronoun)	their
she (subject pronoun)	her		
her (object pronoun)	her		
it (subject/object pronoun)	its		

Numbers

Numbers are determiners, too. Numbers are used **before nouns** to tell you how many people or things there are.

Our family has **two** dogs.

There are **twelve** months in the year.

We bought **three** pizzas.

My grandfather lived for **a hundred** years.

Using Determiners Together

> You can use quantifying determiners with each other and with numbers.

Some people like winter but **many more** people prefer summer.

There's **a little less** space in this cupboard than in that one.

There are **five fewer** children in my class than in your class.

> Use **of** between a quantifying determiner and another kind of determiner.

I don't like **any of these** drinks.

Some of my friends don't like country music.

Each of the boys answered the question correctly.

I've had **enough of your** bad behavior!

Five of these girls are taller than **any of the** boys.

> The quantifying determiner **all** may be used with or without **of**. For example you can say:

We ate **all of** the food in the fridge.	*or*	We ate **all** the food in the fridge.
He spends **all of** his time playing football.	*or*	He spends **all** his time playing football.
She likes **all of** my friends.	*or*	She likes **all** my friends.

Exercise 1

Read the following passage. Write the correct **article** in the blank spaces. If no article is needed, leave the space blank. The first one has been done for you.

John lives in _____an_____ apartment with his mom, dad and sister Katy. _____ apartment has three bedrooms, _____ kitchen, _____ bathroom and _____ living room. John's mom works in _____ office and his dad stays at _____ home and looks after _____ apartment. He spends much of his time in _____ kitchen, preparing meals. John and Katy help their dad with _____ housework. John likes using _____ vacuum cleaner and Katy likes to sweep _____ floor. Dad gives John and Katy money when they help him. They usually spend the money on _____ computer games!

Exercise 2

Notice the **determiners** in the following passage. What kind of determiners are they? Put a **D** in the box after a demonstrative determiner, a **Q** after a quantifying determiner, an **I** after an interrogative determiner, a **P** after a possessive determiner and an **N** after a number.

Sally is my ☐ friend. We play together every ☐ day. I usually go to her ☐ house to play. Her ☐ parents are very nice, but she has two ☐ brothers who sometimes spoil our ☐ games. Last week, her ☐ brothers pulled my ☐ hair. Sally's mom was very angry with them. "Stop behaving in that ☐ rough way!" she shouted. I'm glad I don't have any ☐ brothers.

5 Verbs and Tenses

Most verbs describe actions, so they are called **action verbs**. Action verbs tell what people or things are doing. Here are some common action verbs.

drink	look	jump	swim	fall
eat	shout	walk	throw	climb
laugh	run	sit	catch	dance

Subject and Verb Agreement

When you use a verb, you have to say who or what is doing the action. This 'who or what' is the **subject** of the verb. The subject and the verb match each other. You say that the subject and the verb *agree* when they match each other.

▶ Use a **singular verb** if the subject is a **singular noun**. For example, the subjects 'my dad' or 'our school', or any of the pronouns **he**, **she** or **it**, require a singular verb. Most singular verbs end in **s**. Look at the subjects and their verbs in these examples. The subjects are in bold and the verbs are in color.

He always drinks milk when he's hot.

She eats bananas for breakfast.

Mom walks to work every day.

My sister dances like a professional dancer.

The baby falls when **she** tries to walk.

Our cat climbs the trees in our garden.

This form of the verb is called the **third person singular**. You use it when the subject of the verb is not you or the person you are speaking to, but some other person—a third person—or a thing.

Here are some more **third person singular verbs** that end in **s**.

plays	sings	shines	rides	smiles
draws	paints	blows	thinks	stops
reads	rains	travels	talks	starts

The third person singular form of some verbs is made by adding **es** at the end. Some examples are verbs that end in **sh, ch, ss, x, zz** and **o**.

bru**shes**	wat**ches**	ki**sses**	fi**xes**
ru**shes**	rea**ches**	mi**sses**	mi**xes**
poli**shes**	tea**ches**	pa**sses**	buz**zes**
cra**shes**	cat**ches**	pre**sses**	d**oes**
wa**shes**	tou**ches**	dre**sses**	g**oes**

Here are some sentences with verbs in their **third person singular form**. The subjects are in bold and the verbs are in color.

She always brushes her teeth at bedtime.

Dad polishes his shoes until they shine.

My brother watches television after school.

Kim catches the ball with one hand.

Dad mixes flour and water when he makes bread.

The bee buzzes around the flowers.

My friend Sanjay goes to the same school as I do.

How do you make the third person singular form of most verbs that end in **y**? Usually, you just change the **y** to an **i** and then add **es**.

carry – carr**ies**	hurry – hurr**ies**	copy – cop**ies**
cry – cr**ies**	fly – fl**ies**	marry – marr**ies**
study – stud**ies**	worry – worr**ies**	bully – bull**ies**

A cat carries its kitten with its mouth.

Mr. Chen hurries to work every morning.

The baby cries a lot at night.

This plane flies to the island every day.

Alice tries hard at school.

She copies all the questions in her notebook.

▶ Some verbs that end in **y** have **a vowel before the y**. Just add an **s** at the end of these words to make the third person singular form.

buy – buy**s**	say – say**s**	pray – pray**s**
pay – pay**s**	annoy – annoy**s**	stay – stay**s**

Mom buys bread at the supermarket.

Mr. Carter pays all his bills with a credit card.

My friend says he has a salt-water aquarium.

She annoys me with her silly jokes.

Anna stays with her aunt on weekends.

▶ If the subject of a verb is a **plural noun**, such as "Mom and Dad" or "our teachers", use a **plural verb**. Do not add **s**, **es** or **ies** to plural verbs. Plural verbs are also used with the pronouns **I**, **we**, **you** and **they**.

Mom and Dad love us.

My sisters listen to music a lot.

The stars shine brightly on a clear night.

Some people drink tea.

I like juicy hamburgers.

We learn interesting things at school.

You all know the words to this song, children.

They always walk home from school together.

▶ Suppose the subject of a noun refers to a **group of people**. Depending on the meaning of the sentence, you may use either a singular or a plural verb.

The audience was enjoying the play.
The audience have all gone home.

The class has thirty students.
The class are handing in their papers.

The band is performing until midnight.
The band were arguing among themselves.

Notes

Words that refer to groups of people or animals are called **collective nouns**. Here are some more examples:

crowd	committee	herd
crew	litter	flock

Transitive and Intransitive Verbs

▶ Some verbs have **an object**. The object of a verb is the person or thing that is affected by the **action** of the verb. Look at this sentence:

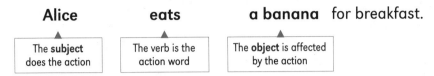

Alice	**eats**	**a banana** for breakfast.
The **subject** does the action	The verb is the action word	The **object** is affected by the action

The **subject** of the verb is **Alice**. She is the person who does the action: **she eats**. The **object** of the verb is **a banana**. **A banana** is affected by the action of the verb. So in this sentence, the object of the verb 'eat ' is 'a banana'. Verbs that have objects are called **transitive verbs**.

Here are some sentences with **transitive verbs**. The verbs are printed in bold and their objects are printed in color.

John **likes** apples.

My sister **cooks** all our meals.

Dad **buys** tea at the market.

Sam **knows** the answer to the question.

My brother **rides** his bike in the street.

Mom **writes** stories in her spare time.

▶ Some verbs don't have an object. A verb that does not have an object is called an **intransitive verb**. Here are some sentences with **intransitive verbs**.

In China, lots of people **walk** to work.

The boys **play** in the yard after school.

Mr. Carter always **drives** very carefully.

Doris **is** a very successful businesswoman.

Michael and I both entered the race. He **won** but I **lost**.

▶ Some verbs can be either transitive or intransitive. Notice that the transitive meaning and the intransitive meaning are sometimes different.

transitive verbs	intransitive verbs
The pilot **flies** the plane very well.	Eagles **fly** high in the sky.
The boys **play** football on weekends.	The boys **play** in the yard on weekends.
My mom **runs** her own company.	My mom **runs** in the park for fun.
We **walk** the dog every evening.	We **walk** on the beach every evening.

*Read the following sentences. Underline the **verb** in each sentence.*

1. We live in an apartment on the boulevard.

2. Some children learn very fast.

3. We go for swimming lessons on Sunday.

4. I like my new bike.

5. Babies sometimes sleep during the day.

6. My dad buys a newspaper every morning.

7. These dolls belong to Kathleen.

8. I often walk to school with my dad.

9. My sister plays the piano very well.

10. Sarah sometimes reads in bed at night.

*Fill in the blank spaces with the **third person singular form** of the verbs in parentheses.*

Example: Ali _____looks_____ (**look**) sad today.

1. Sumiko _____ (**speak**) English very well.

2. Mr. Kim _____ (**come**) to school on his motorbike.

3. My neighbor's dog _____ (**bark**) very loudly.

4. My little brother always _____ (**brush**) his teeth properly.

5. Dad is so tall that his head almost _____ (**touch**) the ceiling.

6. Our dog _____ (**catch**) the ball in its teeth.

7. Mom _____ (**mix**) vinegar and oil to make salad dressing.

8. Sally _____ (**try**) not to disturb her brother when he's reading.

9. Dad _____ (**buy**) his newspaper from the store on the corner.

10. Her music _____ (**annoy**) me when I'm doing my homework.

Exercise 3

Underline the verbs in the following sentences. Then show whether the verb is transitive or intransitive by putting a checkmark (✓) in the correct box. Remember that depending on the meaning, some verbs can be either transitive or intransitive. For each of the transitive verbs you have marked, write the object of the verb on the lines. The first one is done for you.

	intransitive verb	transitive verb	object
1. My brother and I often play chess.		✓	chess
2. Mom and Dad work in the garden on weekends.			
3. The library closes at 5 P.M.			
4. Mr. Ross drives his car very carefully.			
5. The cat jumped over the wall.			
6. My sister likes her new jeans.			
7. Grandad walks the dog every evening.			
8. Will you come with me to the shop?			
9. The boys are skating in the park.			
10. Dad is making sandwiches.			
11. The children went to bed.			
12. We buy our food at the supermarket.			
13. Sally found a good hiding place.			
14. They are learning to speak English.			
15. Anna was reading an interesting book.			
16. On weekends, I usually go to the beach with Dad.			
17. The cat is sleeping under the tree.			
18. They pushed the cart into the shed.			

The Simple Present Tense

▶ Verbs have forms called **tenses** that tell you *when* the action happens. If the **action happens regularly, sometimes** or **never**, use the **simple present tense.**

> We always **wash** our hands before meals.
>
> Joe sometimes **lends** me his bike.
>
> Dad **jogs** in the park every day.
>
> We often **go** to the movies on Satrurday.
>
> Mr. Ross **takes** a train to work.

▶ The simple present tense is also used to state **facts.**

> The sun **rises** every morning.
>
> Penguins **live** in the Antarctica.
>
> Dogs **love** playing in water.
>
> The earth **goes** around the sun.
>
> Australia **is** an island.

▶ Use the simple present tense to tell the events of **a story that is happening now.**

> I **arrive** at school. I **see** another girl crying. I **ask** her why she **is** sad. She **says** she **has**n't got any friends to play with. I **tell** her that she **can play** with me.

▶ Use the simple present tense to talk about **things that will happen in the future.**

> My little sister **starts** school tomorrow.
>
> The new supermarket **opens** this Friday.
>
> Next week I **go** on holiday to Japan.
>
> We **fly** to London on Sunday.
>
> The train **leaves** in five minutes.
>
> My family **moves** to a new house next month.

am, is *and* are

The words **am**, **is** and **are** are the simple present forms of the verb **be**.

- Use **am** with the pronoun I.

- Use **is** with **singular nouns** like 'my dad' and 'the teacher', and with the pronouns **he**, **she** and **it**.

- Use **are** with **plural nouns** like 'my parents' and 'Jenny and Mary', and with the pronouns **we**, **you** and **they**.

I am twelve.	**The children** are asleep.
I am in the garden.	**Computers** are very expensive.
My mom is very tired today.	**My brother and I** are upstairs.
The teacher is tall.	**We** are in our bedrooms.
She is also pretty.	**You** are my best friend.
Our dog is black.	**You and David** are my best friends.

Here is a table to help you remember how to use **is**, **am** and **are**.

	singular	plural
first person	I **am**	we **are**
second person	you **are**	you **are**
third person	he **is**	they **are**
	she **is**	they **are**
	it **is**	they **are**

N o t e s

There are short ways of saying and writing **am**, **is** and **are** with pronouns. These short forms are called contractions.

full form	short form
I am	I'm
you are	you're
he is	he's
she is	she's
it is	it's
we are	we're
they are	they're

You can use these contractions to replace **am**, **is** and **are** when they are used with **not**:

full form	short form
I am not	I'm not
he is not	he isn't
she is not	she isn't
it is not	it isn't
we are not	we aren't
you are not	you aren't
they are not	they aren't

there is *and* there are

Use **there** with **is** and **are** to say what exists or what you can have. Use **there is** with **singular nouns**, and **there are** with **plural nouns**.

There is a tree in our garden.

There is a girl called Farah in my class.

There is fish for dinner.

There is nothing to do when it rains.

There's a cat sitting on the bench.

There's a boy in my class who can walk on his hands.

There are cows in the field.

There are some very big ships in the harbor today.

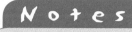

Notes

The contraction for **there is** is **there's**.

Exercise 4

*Look at the pairs of subjects and verbs below. Then write a sentence using each subject with the **simple present** form of the verb. Remember that you can also use the simple present tense to talk about the future.*

Example: Dad goes to work on his bike.

subject	verb
1. Dad	go _____
2. My brother	ride _____
3. The dog	watch _____
4. The bus	leave _____
5. Tom and Sam	buy _____
6. We	eat _____
7. Aunt Grace	come _____
8. Our neighbor	like _____
9. The boys	start _____
10. My family	travel _____

Complete the following sentences by writing *am*, *is* or *are* in the blank spaces.

1. The weather _____ beautiful today.

2. All the children _____ on the playground.

3. Boys! You _____ always late for class.

4. _____ you on the basketball team, too?

5. Nobody in my class _____ interested in football.

6. _____ this computer more expensive than that one?

7. Sally _____ my best friend.

8. Mom and Dad _____ downstairs watching television.

9. Paul and Henry _____ in the computer room.

10. The Eiffel Tower _____ the tallest monument in Paris.

Exercise 6

Read the following passage. Fill in *there's*, *there are*, *there isn't* or *there aren't* in the blank spaces.

I like playing in our park because _____ some great things to play on.

_____ a big chute to slide on and a huge sandbox to play in. _____

also some swings. Dogs are not allowed in the park so _____ no dogs to bother us.

_____ also a lot of space for us to run around. It sometimes gets hot because

_____ many trees to give shade, but _____ a fountain where we can drink

water. It's the best place in the town for children. _____ another place as good as

the park.

Rewrite the following sentences using contractions. The first one has already been done to help you.

1. It is another sunny day today.

   It's another sunny day today.

2. This is my sister. She is five.

   _____

3. I am not very interested in sports.

   _____

4. She is not my best friend. You are my best friend.

   _____

5. Cats are not as noisy as dogs.

   _____

6. We are busy doing our homework.

   _____

7. She is busy cleaning the car in the garage.

   _____

8. Our teacher is not very tall.

   _____

9. My parents are not home from work yet.

   _____

10. My friend is not very good at math.

    _____

The Present Progressive Tense

The present progressive tense is used to talk about **things that are continuing to happen**.

▶ Make the present progressive tense by using **am**, **is** or **are** with a verb that ends in **ing**.

I **am learning** how to swim.

I **am eating** my lunch.

I **am watching** television.

She **is reading** a book.

Dad **is baking** a cake.

My sister **is listening** to music.

Uncle David **is cleaning** his car.

The dog **is barking** in the garden.

We **are singing** our favorite song.

My brother and I **are playing** a computer game.

The teachers **are showing** us a film.

They **are bringing** a television set into the classroom.

> **N o t e s**
>
> The **ing** form of a verb is called the **present participle**. You use the **present participle** with **am**, **is** or **are** to make the present progressive tense.
>
> am + watch**ing**
>   (present participle)
>
> is + listen**ing**
>   (present participle)
>
> are + play**ing**
>   (present participle)

▶ The present progressive tense is also used to talk about **things that are planned for the future**.

I **am going** to the library tomorrow.

My sister **is giving** me her bike when she gets her new one.

We can't go to the movies tomorrow because my mom **is working**.

We **are having** a barbecue on Sunday.

All my friends **are coming** to my party next week.

We**'re taking** my cousin to the zoo later today.

63

Fill in the blank spaces with the present progressive tense of the verbs in parentheses. Try to use contractions such as **I'm**, **she's** and **they're** where you can.

1. We _____ (**go**) to the zoo tomorrow.

2. He _____ (**fix**) my bike in the garage.

3. I _____ (**help**) Mom in the kitchen.

4. My sister and I _____ (**watch**) television in our bedroom.

5. The train _____ (**leave**) in ten minutes.

6. They _____ (**come**) with us to the museum.

7. We _____ (**paint**) some pictures for Aunt Susan.

8. The boys and girls _____ (**dance**) in the hall.

9. The cat _____ (**chase**) some birds.

10. My brother _____ (**tickle**) me.

Complete the following sentences with either 1) the **simple present form** of the verb, or 2) the **present progressive form** of the verb.

1. The teacher always _____ (**give**) us interesting project work.

2. The wind _____ (**blow**) very strongly today.

3. I _____ (**like**) chocolate ice cream.

4. Be quiet! We _____ (**try**) to listen to the radio.

5. Let's go inside now. It _____ (**begin**) to rain.

6. Penguins _____ (**eat**) fish.

7. Dad never _____ (**let**) us play in the street when it's dark.

8. The children _____ (**go**) swimming every day.

9. We're trying to catch the ball that _____ (**roll**) down the hill.

10. My teacher _____ (**know**) a lot about plants and animals.

The Simple Past Tense

▶ Use the simple past tense to talk about **things that happened in the past**. The simple past tense is usually made by adding **ed** to the verb.

I opened the door and **looked** inside.

The plane **landed** ten minutes ago.

My cousin **visited** us last summer.

We **walked** to school yesterday.

She **laughed** when I told her the joke.

▶ If a verb ends in **e**, just add **d** to make the simple past tense.

Who **closed** all the windows?

We **lived** in that house when I was a baby.

She **smiled** when she saw me.

We **raced** each other on our bikes.

▶ If a verb ends in **y**, change the **y** to **i** before adding **ed**.

I **carried** my mom's shopping bag.

My brother **cried** when he fell off his bike.

We **hurried** to the station to catch the train.

Dad **tried** to help me with my homework.

▶ With some **short verbs** that end in a consonant, you must double the consonant before adding **ed**.

I climbed over the fence and **ripped** my shirt.

The stranger **grabbed** my arm.

The dog **wagged** its tail when it saw the biscuits.

He **slammed** the door and walked off angrily.

was *and* were

The words **was** and **were** are the simple past forms of the verb **be**.

■ **Was** is the simple past form of **am** and **is**. Use **was** with **singular nouns** like 'my dad' and 'the teacher', and with the pronouns **he**, **she** and **it**.

■ **Were** is the simple past form of **are**. Use **were** with **plural nouns** like 'my parents' and 'Jenny and Mary', and with the pronouns **we**, **you** and **they**.

Ten years ago, I **was** only a baby.

When I **was** younger, I played with teddy bears.

My friend **was** ill yesterday.

Mom **was** angry when she saw the broken vase.

It **was** very wet on Monday.

It **was** six o'clock when we got home.

We **were** away on vacation last month.

John and I **were** in the garden.

You **were** nasty to me!

You and Sally **were** not at school yesterday.

Dinosaurs **were** prehistoric animals.

Those **were** my best jeans.

Here is a table to help you remember how to use **was** and **were**.

	singular	plural
first person	I was	we were
second person	you were	you were
third person	he was	they were
	she was	they were
	it was	they were

N o t e s

You may use these contractions when you are combining **was** and **were** with **not**.

full form	short form
I was not	I wasn't
he was not	he wasn't
she was not	she wasn't
it was not	it wasn't
we were not	we weren't
you were not	you weren't
they were not	they weren't

Irregular Verbs

▶ Many common verbs have unusual present and past tense forms. These are called **irregular verbs**.

Remember that the simple past tense of most verbs is made by adding **ed** at the end: **look** becomes **looked**. Notice that the simple past tense of these common **irregular verbs** is quite different.

irregular verb	simple past tense	irregular verb	simple past tense
break	broke	keep	kept
bring	brought	kneel	knelt
buy	bought	know	knew
catch	caught	leave	left
come	came	lose	lost
do	did	meet	met
fall	fell	ring	rang
feed	fed	run	ran
feel	felt	see	saw
fly	flew	sell	sold
get	got	sleep	slept
go	went	speak	spoke
have	had	write	wrote

▶ The simple past tense of other **irregular verbs** does not change at all.

verb	simple past tense	example
cost	cost	I bought a new CD. It **cost** twenty dollars.
cut	cut	My brother **cut** his finger this morning.
hit	hit	She **hit** the ball into a neighbor's garden.
hurt	hurt	I **hurt** my leg when I jumped off the wall.
let	let	Mom opened the door and **let** us in.
put	put	The tea tasted horrible because I **put** too much sugar in it.
read	read	Dad **read** us a story last night.

Exercise 10

Write each past tense verb below under the correct heading.

laughed	lived	smiled	landed
cried	pinned	hurried	played
hopped	tried	grabbed	raced

verb + *ed*	verb + *d*	double the last letter + *ed*	change *y* to *i* and add *ed*

Exercise 11

Complete the sentences with the simple past tense of the verbs in parentheses.

1. The boys _____ (**whisper**) secrets to each other.

2. Uncle Ben _____ (**hurry**) to catch his bus.

3. We _____ (**return**) our books to the library.

4. She _____ (**kiss**) the frog and it _____ (**change**) into a prince.

5. Someone _____ (**tap**) me on the shoulder.

6. The baby _____ (**cry**) when we took her toy away.

7. John _____ (**pin**) the badge onto his jacket.

8. Two doctors _____ (**rush**) into the room.

9. This is the house that we _____ (**live**) in when I was younger.

10. Grandad _____ (**lower**) himself into the chair.

Exercise 12

*Write **was** or **were** in the blank spaces in the following passage.*

It _____ a beautiful summer's day and there _____ n't a cloud in the sky.

Mom, Dad and I _____ all in the garden. Dad _____ in the vegetable

garden planting some seeds and Mom and I _____ busy with other jobs. The

sun _____ hot and soon I _____ feeling very tired. Mom and Dad

_____ n't tired at all. They went on working for a long time. I _____

glad when it _____ time to go inside and have a drink.

Exercise 13

*Draw a circle around the correct **past tense verb** in each sentence below.*

1. I (**losed** / **lost**) my watch in the park.

2. David (**hurt** / **hurted**) his knee when he (**falled** / **fell**).

3. I kicked the ball hard and it (**breaked** / **broke**) a window.

4. My new shoes (**cost** / **costed**) a lot of money.

5. I (**getted** / **got**) this book from the library.

6. We had a garage where we (**keeped** / **kept**) our car.

7. Ali (**shew** / **showed**) me the cut on his knee.

8. The glass (**falled** / **fell**) off the table and (**breaked** / **broke**).

9. We (**selled** / **sold**) our old car and (**buyed** / **bought**) a new one.

10. The bell (**ringed** / **rang**) and we all (**goed** / **went**) into school.

11. The dog (**catched** / **caught**) the ball in its mouth.

12. The man (**kneeled** / **knelt**) down to talk to the little boy.

13. I (**meeted** / **met**) my friend in the park.

14. Our cat (**runned** / **ran**) onto the road in front of a car.

15. Jane (**writed** / **wrote**) a letter to her best friend.

The Past Progressive Tense

▶ Use the past progressive tense to talk about **things that were happening** in the past and had not stopped happening. They were continuing.

To make the past progressive tense, use **was** or **were** and a verb that ends in **ing**.

> I **was watching** television.
>
> Ben **was finishing** his homework.
>
> She **was putting** her books into her schoolbag.
>
> Jenny and I **were tidying** the classroom.
>
> We **were** all **dancing** at the party.
>
> You **weren't listening** to the teacher.
>
> Some boys **were looking** out of the window.

> ### N o t e s
>
> The **ing** form of a verb is called the **present participle**. You use the present participles with **was** or **were** to make the past progressive tense:
>
> **was** + cleaning
> *(present participle)*
>
> **were** + listening
> *(present participle)*

▶ You can also use the past progressive tense to say **what was happening when something else happened.**

> Sam **was doing** his math homework when the phone rang.
>
> Dad **was cooking** our dinner when I got home.
>
> When I saw Joe, he **was looking** for his dog.
>
> We **were** all **enjoying** the movie when the power went out.
>
> What **were** they **doing** when the bell rang?

Exercise 14

*Complete the sentences with the **past progressive tense** of the verbs in parentheses.*

1. At the block party lots of people _____ (**dance**) in the street.

2. I _____ (**sit**) in my bedroom reading a book.

3. Someone _____ (**make**) a very loud noise in the street.

4. Why _____ you all _____ (**laugh**) when I came in?

5. Mike and John _____ (**wash**) their paintbrushes.

6. Sally _____ (**practice**) the piano.

7. I ran so fast that my heart _____ (**beat**) really hard.

8. Our neighbors _____ (**have**) a barbecue.

have, has *and* had

▶ The verb **have** is used to say **what people own or possess**.

■ Use **have** with the pronouns I, **we**, **you** and **they**, and with **plural nouns** such as 'my parents' and 'Tom and Susan'.

■ Use **has** with the pronouns **he**, **she** and **it**, and with **singular nouns** such as 'my dad' and 'the teacher'.

I **have** two brothers and one sister.

Monkeys **have** long tails.

My sister and I **have** a swing in our garden.

John **has** a big brother.

Sally **has** a pretty face.

An elephant **has** a long trunk. It also **has** big ears.

His brother **has** dark hair.

Our apartment **has** big windows.

> ### N o t e s
> The words **have** and **has** are the simple present forms of the verb **have**.

▶ Use **have** to talk about **things that people do or get**.

I can't play football because I **have** a broken leg.

We **have** art lessons on Mondays.

You **have** a stain on your shirt.

They **have** the desks nearest the teacher.

Peter **has** a sore knee.

▶ You also use **have** to talk about **things that people eat**.

We usually **have** lunch at school.

Mom and Dad sometimes **have** their breakfast in bed.

Jenny often **has** sandwiches for lunch.

She sometimes **has** cola to drink.

Here is a table to help you remember how to use **have** and **has**.

	singular	plural
first person	I have	we have
second person	you have	you have
third person	he has	they have
	she has	they have
	it has	they have

The simple past tense form of **have** and **has** is **had**.

I **had** a big toy car when I was small.

It was sunny so **we had** lunch in the garden.

They **had** a wonderful holiday in Europe.

Sally and I had chicken for dinner.

The boys had a fight in the playground.

Dad had a sore back yesterday.

She had long hair when I saw her a year ago.

Our cat had three kittens last week.

Use **had** when you're talking about **wishes**.

I **wish** I **had** a new bike.

Kathleen **wishes** she **had** a big sister.

Dad **wishes** he **had** a bigger garage.

The boys **wish** they **had** more space to play football in.

You can make the negative with **didn't have**.

I **wish** I **didn't have** so much homework.

Jack **wishes** he **didn't have** a broken leg.

Dad **wishes** he **didn't have** to work on weekends.

Do you **wish** you **didn't have** English classes today?

The Present Perfect Tense

The present perfect tense shows action in the indefinite past. The present perfect tense is also used to show action begun in the past and continuing into the present.

To make the present perfect tense, use **have** or **has** and a verb that ends in **ed**.

We **have lived** in this house for five years.
(= *and we still live there*)

Your plane **has** already **landed**.
(= *and it's still on the ground*)

She **has dirtied** her new shoes.
(= *she made them dirty and they're still dirty*)

The teacher **has pinned** a notice on the board.
(= *and the notice is still there*)

You don't need your key. I**'ve** already **opened**
the door. (= *and it's still open*)

> **N o t e s**
>
> The **ed** form of a verb is called the **past participle** when it is used with **has** or **have** to make the present perfect tense:
>
> **have** + land**ed**
> (*past participle*)
>
> **has** + open**ed**
> (*past participle*)

Irregular Past Participles

Remember that irregular verbs don't have a simple past form that ends in -ed.

> **Irregular verbs** also have unusual **past participles** that don't end in -ed. The past participle of some verbs is the same as the simple past tense.

irregular verb	simple past tense	past participle
fight	fought	fought
have	had	had
lose	lost	lost
teach	taught	taught
win	won	won

Here are more examples of **irregular past participles**.

irregular verb	simple past tense	past participle	example
keep	kept	kept	I **have kept** the letter you sent me.
catch	caught	caught	The police **have caught** the thieves.
bring	brought	brought	Maggie **has brought** her favorite CD to school.
make	made	made	The children **have made** a birthday card for their mom.
sell	sold	sold	They'**ve sold** their car and now they
buy	bought	bought	**have bought** motorcycles.

Some common **irregular verbs** have a past participle that is **different** from the simple past tense.

irregular verb	simple past form	past participle	example
be	was	been	Anna **has been** my best friend for years.
break	broke	broken	I'm sorry, I'**ve broken** your pencil.
do	did	done	Jack **has** already **done** his homework.
draw	drew	drawn	We'**ve drawn** a picture for you, Mom.
drink	drank	drunk	**Have** you **drunk** all your orange juice?
eat	ate	eaten	Someone **has eaten** all the chocolates.
fall	fell	fallen	One of the pictures has **fallen** off the wall.
go	went	gone	I'm sorry, but your train **has** already **gone**.
know	knew	known	I'**ve known** Michael for two years.
see	saw	seen	Kathleen **has** already **seen** that movie.
speak	spoke	spoken	Miss Hill **has spoken** to the principal about the problem.

Some **irregular verbs** have a past participle that **does not change** at all.

irregular verb	past participle	example
cut	cut	I'**ve cut** my finger and it's bleeding badly.
hit	hit	The children next door **have hit** their ball into the busy street.
cost	cost	This vacation **has cost** us hundreds of dollars already.
read	read	Dad **hasn't read** my school report yet.
hurt	hurt	Can Anna sit down? She'**s hurt** her leg.
put	put	**Have** you **put** any sugar in my tea?

Exercise 15

*Complete the following sentences with **has** or **have**.*

1. My dog _____ a long shiny coat.

2. Our teacher _____ a very kind face.

3. You _____ a lot of homework to do.

4. Sam and I _____ desks near the front of the class.

5. Paul _____ two brothers and a sister.

6. My friend Andy _____ a big house.

7. Mice _____ long tails.

8. Most dogs _____ sharp teeth.

9. I _____ more toys than my friend _____.

10. These flowers _____ a strange smell.

*Complete the sentence with the **present perfect tense** of the verbs in parentheses.*

1. The children _____ (**make**) the house very messy.

2. I _____ (**see**) that actor in several movies.

3. The boys _____ (**drink**) all the soda in the refrigerator.

4. Our dog _____ (**hurt**) its leg.

5. One of the workmen _____ (**fall**) off his ladder.

6. She's sad because her friends _____ (**go**) to the park without her.

7. Dad _____ (**have**) a shower already.

8. I've been shouting so much that I _____ (**lose**) my voice.

9. My sister's boyfriend _____ (**buy**) her a diamond ring.

10. Alan _____ (**do**) this jigsaw puzzle so many times that he could do it with his eyes shut.

*Draw a circle around the correct **past participle** in each sentence below.*

1. Your child has (**broke/broken**) my window!

2. Have you (**eaten/ate**) all your dinner?

3. I have (**known/knew**) Sally since we were in kindergarden.

4. Michael has (**drew/drawn**) a picture for his grandad.

5. The new girl seems nice, but I haven't (**spoke/spoken**) to her yet.

6. We've (**drank/drunk**) all the milk.

7. The ball has (**went/gone**) over the garden fence.

8. Has Tom (**did/done**) all his homework?

9. You have (**been/was**) late for school every day this week.

10. Help! I've (**fell/fallen**) down a hole!

The Future Tense

▶ To show future action use the verbs **shall** and **will** with another verb that describes the action.

- ■ You can use either **shall** or **will** with the pronouns **I** and **we**.

- ■ Use **will** with the pronouns **you**, **he**, **she**, **it** and **they**.

- ■ **Will** is also used with **singular nouns** like 'my dad' and with **plural nouns** like 'all the boys in my class'.

I **shall do** my homework after dinner.

I **will miss** you when you leave.

We **shall take** the dog for a walk later.

We **will visit** Grandma this weekend.

He **will be** home later.

She **will help** us cook the food for the party.

It **will** soon **be** dark outside.

I think it **will be** sunny tomorrow.

I expect they **will give** you a present.

Mom **will be** very pleased with you.

Your plant **will die** without water.

The school **will** soon **need** a lot of repairs.

John and I **shall be** glad when the exams are over.

Bill and Kim **will be** late for school if they don't hurry.

Notes

You can shorten **shall** and **will** as **'ll** when you use these words with pronouns:

full form	contraction
I shall, I will	I'll
we shall, we will	we'll
you will	you'll
he will	he'll
she will	she'll
it will	it'll
they will	they'll

▶ To make the negative form, use **will** and **shall** with **not**. The contraction for **will not** is **won't**.

I **will not** help you unless you help me first.

It **won't** be very sunny again until next summer.

You **won't** like this food. It's horrible!

We **shall not** go to the party without you.

To talk about **facts in the future** or **plans that will not change**, use the **simple present tense.**

Tomorrow **is** Sunday.

Summer vacation **ends** on Friday.

The new library **opens** next week.

We **fly** to Paris on Wednesday.

You can also talk about **plans for the future** and other **future happenings** by using **be going to** and another verb. Remember to:

- Use **am** and **was** with the pronoun **I.**

- Use **is** and **was** with the pronouns **he, she** and **it,** and with **singular nouns** like 'my mom' and 'the teacher'.

- Use **are** and **were** with the pronouns **we, you** and **they,** and with **plural nouns** like 'my friends' and 'John and Sally'.

I **am going to visit** my cousin tomorrow.

I **am going to see** the new Star Wars movie next week.

My friend John **is going to move** to Chicago next year.

Dad **is going to buy** me a skateboard.

Aunt Jane **is going to have** another baby soon.

It **is going to be** windy tomorrow.

I hope someone **is going to fix** the television soon.

You **are going to help** me, aren't you?

My friends **are going to teach** me how to play chess.

Mom and Dad **are going to buy** a new computer.

Your books **are going to fall** off the shelf if you're not careful.

Are you **going to read** your book now?

Exercise 18

Decide whether **shall** and **will** are used correctly in each sentence. Put a checkmark ✓ in the box for a correct use and an x ☒ in the box for an incorrect use.

1. My dad will ☐ be home later.

2. I will ☐ never forget my days at school.

3. Tom and Kumar shall ☐ come with us.

4. The weather report says that it shall ☐ be sunny again tomorrow.

5. We will ☐ miss my cousins when they leave.

6. Raj and I shall ☐ feel happier when the exams are over.

7. It will ☐ be late when we arrive in London.

8. I shall ☐ stay awake all night and watch for Santa Claus.

9. My grandparents shall ☐ enjoy coming to our house for Christmas.

10. The winter holidays shall ☐ give us all a good rest.

Exercise 19

Read the pairs of subjects and verbs below. Then write sentences about future events using the correct form of **be going to**. For example, for the first sentence you could write:

My friend Tom is going to sleep at my house tonight.

	subject	verb	
1.	My friend Tom	sleep	_____
2.	We	ride	_____
3.	The dog	catch	_____
4.	Uncle Andy	come	_____
5.	It	rain	_____
6.	We	eat	_____
7.	Jamal and I	have	_____
8.	The teachers	read	_____

do, does *and* did

The verb **do** is used to talk about actions. The words **do** and **does** are the simple present forms of the verb **do**.

- Use **do** with the pronouns **I**, **we**, **you** and **they**, and with **plural nouns** such as 'my parents' and 'Tom and Susan'.

- Use **does** with the pronouns **he**, **she** and **it**, and with **singular nouns** such as 'my dad' and 'the teacher'.

I always **do** my homework after dinner.

I **do** drawings with colored pencils.

We **do** our shopping at the supermarket.

You **do** magic tricks very well.

They **do** their housework on the weekend.

Mom and Dad **do** the cooking together.

Jim and Alan always **do** well in math tests.

The artist **does** beautiful paintings.

She **does** very interesting work.

He **does** the washing and she **does** the cooking.

Julie always **does** her exercises before breakfast.

My friend **Hannah does** karate at a local gym.

The **vacuum cleaner does** a better job than the broom.

Here is a table to help you remember how to use **do** and **does**.

	singular	plural
first person	I do	we do
second person	you do	you do
third person	he does	they do
	she does	they do
	it does	they do

▶ The simple past form of **do** is **did**.

> I **did** my homework but forgot to take it to school.
>
> Sally **did** her hair in front of the mirror.
>
> The boys **did** very badly in their spelling test.
>
> Paul and Roger **did** some magic tricks for us.
>
> The children **did** the housework while their parents relaxed.

▶ To make the negative form of verbs in the simple present tense, use **do** and **does** with **not**.

> I **do not have** any brothers or sisters.
>
> We **do not want** any more bread, thank you.
>
> My brother and I **do not like** football.
>
> You see beautiful mountains in Scotland but **you do not see** much sunshine.
>
> Mom **does not buy** our food at that supermarket.
>
> Jenny **does not eat** lunch at school because **she does not like** the food.
>
> My cat **does not make** as much noise as your dog.

▶ The simple past tense of **does not** and **do not** is **did not**. The contraction is **didn't**.

> Maggie **did not have** long hair when I first met her.
>
> I got sunburned because I **did not wear** my hat.
>
> The teacher **didn't give** us any homework.
>
> Mom and Dad **didn't buy** me a cell phone for my birthday.
>
> You **didn't take** the dog for a walk last night.

N o t e s

Here are the contractions you can use when **do**, **does** and **did** are used with **not**.

full form	short form	full form	short form
I/we do not	I/we don't	I/we did not	I/we didn't
you do not	you don't	you did not	you didn't
they do not	they don't	they did not	they didn't
he/she/it does not	he/she/it doesn't	he/she/it did not	he/she/it didn't

Exercise 20

Complete the following sentences with do, does or did.

1. I always _____ my homework in my room.

2. Mom and Dad usually _____ the laundry together.

3. You _____ the same math problems last week.

4. We always _____ our shopping at the farmers' market.

5. The children _____ their work quietly while the teacher looks at their

   homework.

6. Uncle David _____ magic tricks when he comes to visit.

7. Last night, Mom _____ her exercises before bedtime.

8. Anna played the piano and Rachel _____ a lively dance.

9. Kamal always _____ well in math tests.

10. If John _____ the cooking, will you _____ the dishes?

Exercise 21

Complete the following sentences with the contractions don't, doesn't or didn't.

1. Katy _____ go to school on the bus.

2. I _____ like chocolate ice cream.

3. If the weather _____ improve, we'll have the party indoors.

4. _____ worry about the mess. It does not matter.

5. I _____ answer all the questions on the math test.

6. Mom and Dad _____ work on weekends.

7. My sister and I _____ visit Grandma last Sunday.

8. My friend John _____ finish his homework yesterday.

9. Our neighbors _____ like dogs very much.

10. Our teacher _____ speak Japanese.

The Infinitive

The **infinitive** is the base form of a verb. It is often preceded by the word **to**.

▶ Infinitives often appear **after other verbs**.

The rain began **to fall**.

Sally and I agreed **to meet** this afternoon.

I've arranged **to see** the doctor at 3 o'clock.

I hope **to visit** Disneyland someday.

I like **to ride** my bike in the street.

My parents have decided **to buy** a new car.

Paul is learning **to swim**.

I didn't mean **to upset** you.

▶ Some verbs have an **object before the infinitive**. In these examples the objects are printed in color.

Simon asked me **to help** him.

The teacher told us not **to run** in the corridor.

Susie persuaded her friends **to play** on the team.

The manager allowed the staff **to leave** early.

▶ Infinitives often appear **after adjectives**. In these examples the adjectives are printed in color.

The boys were afraid **to cross** the busy road.

I'm very pleased **to see** you again.

This problem will be difficult **to solve**.

The shelf is too high **to reach**.

Don't you think it's rude **to ignore** the new girl in class?

The experiment was interesting **to watch**.

You're welcome **to come** with me.

You can also use infinitives **after some nouns and pronouns** to say what you are using something for.

Take **a book to read**.

I phoned for **a taxi to take** us to the airport.

Has everyone got **something to drink**?

I've got lots of nice **clothes to wear**.

Find **a space on the floor to sit in**.

Infinitives sometimes follow words like **how**, **what**, **which** and **where**.

My brother is learning **how to cook**.

I can't decide **which to choose**—the ice cream or the pudding.

I don't know **what to say**.

Sally can't remember **where to hang** her coat.

Infinitives are also used **after helping verbs** such as **will, can, should, may** and **must**. After these helping verbs use infinitives without the word **to**.

I **can swim**.

We think she **will win** the race.

You **must try** harder.

Do you think we **should wait**?

May I **come** in?

> **N o t e s**
>
> The helping verbs **will, can, should, may** and **must** are called **auxiliary verbs**.

The Imperative Form of Verbs

When you give an order or command, use the base form of a verb, such as **give**, **read** or **come**. This base form is called **the imperative**.

Open your books to page 25.

Stop and **look** before you cross the road.

Come to the front of the class.

Show me your homework.

Read the first sentence out loud.

Choose a partner and **stand** in a circle.

▶ **Imperatives** are very direct. To be more polite, you can use **please** before the imperative.

> **Please show** me your homework.

> **Please read** the first sentence out loud.

> **Please come** to the front of the class.

▶ To make negative imperatives, use **do not** or **don't** before the base form of the verb.

> **Do not bring** calculators into the exam room.

> Please **don't change** anything on my computer.

Gerunds

▶ A **gerund** is the **ing** form of a verb used as a noun. Sometimes a gerund is called a **verbal noun** because it comes from a verb.

> **Running** is a good way to keep fit.

> Susan is very good at **drawing**.

> He loves **dancing** and **singing**.

> Have you ever tried **sailing**?

> I don't like **watching television**.

> We enjoyed **visiting our grandparents**.

Notes

Sometimes it is difficult to know whether an **ing** word is a **gerund** or a **present participle**. If you can replace the **ing** word or its phrase with the pronoun **it**, then the word is a gerund. Look again at the examples on the left. Try replacing the words in bold with **it**.

▶ Some gerunds can be used **in front of other nouns**, like adjectives.

a **washing** machine	=	a machine that does washing
a **shopping** bag	=	a bag for carrying your purchases
walking boots	=	boots you wear for walking in the countryside
gardening clothes	=	clothes you wear for gardening

Exercise 22

Look at the following half-sentences that contain adjectives. Complete each sentence with an **infinitive**. For example, for the first sentence you could write:

   I was too afraid to touch the spider.

1. I was too afraid _____.

2. Mom and Dad are happy _____.

3. She seemed very pleased _____.

4. The book was very interesting _____.

5. Is your hand small enough _____?

6. The dog looked too tired _____.

7. The wall was impossible _____.

8. The first question wasn't easy_____.

9. It was embarrassing _____.

10. The sea was warm and wonderful _____.

Exercise 23

Decide whether or not each sentence uses the infinitive correctly. Mark a correct use with a checkmark ✓ , and an incorrect use with an x X .

1. She likes play in the park. ☐

2. The sun was beginning to shine. ☐

3. I decided to help Dad with the dinner. ☐

4. Mom asked me close the window. ☐

5. The teacher warned me to be quiet. ☐

6. I didn't know which tool use. ☐

7. We couldn't decide how many cakes to buy. ☐

8. Can I to watch the TV, Mom? ☐

9. Do you think I should help him? ☐

10. I think I shall to go home now. ☐

Exercise 24

Study the following pairs of verbs and nouns. Then write a sentence using each pair with the verb as an **imperative**. Try to use negatives in some of your sentences. For the first pair, you could write:

Show him the picture.   **or**   Don't show him the picture.

	verb	noun	
1.	show	picture	_____
2.	bring	bike	_____
3.	eat	sandwiches	_____
4.	wash	hands	_____
5.	listen	parents	_____
6.	wait	name	_____
7.	sleep	classroom	_____
8.	make	noise	_____

Exercise 25

Make a **gerund** from each verb below. Then write a sentence using that gerund. For example, the gerund you can make from the first verb is **cycling**. You could write the sentence:

She loves cycling in the countryside.

	verb	gerund
1.	cycle	cycling _____
2.	paint	_____
3.	eat	_____
4.	sleep	_____
5.	watch	_____
6.	bake	_____
7.	fly	_____
8.	cook	_____

6 Auxiliary Verbs

Auxiliary, or helping verbs, are used **before infinitives** to add a different meaning. For example, you use auxiliary verbs to say:

- that someone is able to do something,

- that someone is allowed to do something, or

- that someone has to do something.

The helping verbs are **can, could, would, should, ought to, will, shall, may, might** and **must.**

can *and* could

▶ Use **can** and **could** to say that someone is **able to do something.**

> She **can draw** really good pictures.
>
> Philip **can run** faster than Matt.
>
> **Can** you **ride** a bike?
>
> **Can** you **help** me with my homework?
>
> She **could** already **read** before she started school.
>
> Our teacher said we **could go** home early.
>
> I ran as fast as I **could.**
>
> Sarah **could not come** to the party because she was ill.

> **Notes**
>
> - **Could** is the simple past tense form of **can.**
>
> - When you put **not** after **can,** write it as one word: **cannot.**
>
>   They **cannot find** their way home.
>
> - The contraction of **cannot** is **can't,** and the contraction of **could not** is **couldn't.**
>
>   They **can't find** their way home.
>
>   I'm full. **I can't eat** any more.
>
>   Sarah **couldn't come** to the party because she was ill.

▶ You may also use **can** and **could** to say that someone is **allowed to do something.**

> My mom says you **can come** to our house for dinner.
>
> Dad says I **can't walk** to school on my own.
>
> You **can't go** in there without a ticket.
>
> Mom said I **could have** ice cream after my dinner.
>
> The big sign on the gate said PRIVATE, so we **couldn't** go in.

Can and could are also used for **asking for information or help**, for **offering something**, and for **suggesting something**.

> **Can you tell** me if this train goes to Topeka?
>
> **Could you show** me where the accident happened?
>
> **Could you open** that window, please?
>
> **You can borrow** my pen, if you like.
>
> **Your sister could come** with us, if she wanted to.
>
> **I could lend** you my football.
>
> **We can go** to the library instead.
>
> **You could ask** your dad to help us.
>
> **John can borrow** his brother's skates.

will *and* would

Use **will** and **would** when you are **asking someone to do something**.

> **Will you** please stop making that noise?
>
> **Would you** pass me that book, please?
>
> Please, **will you** close the door?

You can also use **will** and **would** to **offer something** or to **suggest something**.

> **Will I** hold this end of the rope?
>
> **Will I** carry the bag for you?
>
> **Would you** like another drink?
>
> Which cake **would you** like?

N o t e s

The contraction of **will not** is **won't** and the contraction of **would not** is **wouldn't**:

Won't you stay and eat with us?

Wouldn't it be better to wait?

shall *and* should

You can use **shall** and **should** to **ask for advice**, **offer something** and **suggest something**.

> **Should I** bring waterproof clothes?
>
> **Should I** phone the police?
>
> **Shall we** go home now?

> **Shall I** go by car, or will it be better to walk?
>
> **Shall I** help you with that heavy bag?
>
> **You should** try that new French restaurant.

ought to

You use **ought to** to **make strong suggestions** and **talk about someone's duty.**

> You look tired. **You ought to** go to bed early tonight.
>
> **I ought to** get more physical exercise.
>
> **We ought to** lock the door when we leave home.
>
> **You ought to** turn off the computer when you're not using it.
>
> **You ought to** know how to spell your own name.
>
> **The teacher ought to** make his classes more interesting.

must

Use **must** to **talk about things that you have to do.**

> **I must** mail this letter today.
>
> **You must** speak louder. I can't hear you.
>
> **Children must not** play with matches.
>
> Go to bed now. Oh, **must I?**
>
> Why **must I** do my homework tonight?

> ### N o t e s
>
> ■ **Must** keeps the same form in the past tense.
>
> ■ The contraction of **must not** is **mustn't.**
>
> **She mustn't** let the dog sleep on her bed.

may *and* might

▶ Use **may** to **ask if you are allowed** to do something and to **tell someone that they are allowed** to do something.

> "**May I** go out to play now?" "Yes, **you may.**"
>
> **May I** borrow your pen?
>
> Please **may I** see your ticket?
>
> **John may** leave now, but **Sally may not.**
>
> **May Kenny** come with us to the movies?

▶ Use **may** and **might** to **talk about things that are possible or likely.**

> Take an umbrella. **It might** rain.
>
> **I may not** have time to go swimming tonight.
>
> **We might** go to the party later.
>
> If you're not careful, **you may** hurt yourself.
>
> "Are you going to the concert?" "I don't know. **I might** or **I might not.**"

Verb Phrases

A **verb phrase** consists of a **verb** and a preposition such as **after**, **into** and **over**. The **preposition** gives the verb a special meaning.

Here are some sentences that contain phrasal verbs. Read the meanings in parentheses.

Who **looks after** (= *takes care of*) the baby when your parents are at work?

Mike has blond hair and blue eyes. He **takes after** (= *looks like*) his mother.

Dad **bumped into** (= *met by chance*) an old friend at the station.

My sister **is getting into** (= *is starting to be interested in*) pop music.

Is your mom **getting over** (= *recovering from*) her illness?

Some health inspectors came to **look over** (= *inspect*) the factory.

We hoped that the thieves **wouldn't get away with** (= *escape punishment for*) their crime.

I'm going to the store because we**'ve run out of** rice (= *used all our rice*).

N o t e s

Some verb phrases have three parts:

get away with

run out of

Exercise 1

Complete the sentences below by writing ***can*** *or* ***can't*** *on the blanks.*

1. You _____ borrow my book, if you want to.

2. Sam looked everywhere but he _____ find his pencil.

3. Don't help me. I _____ do it by myself.

4. Sandy _____ open the window. She's not tall enough to reach it.

5. "Why _____ John come out to play?" "Because he's ill."

6. This is a film for adults only. Children _____ watch it.

7. _____ you help me with this heavy bag?

8. They've lost the map and _____ find their way back to the hotel.

Exercise 2

Complete the sentences using **would** or **wouldn't** with a verb from the list below. The first one has been done for you.

stop	work	help	take	like
wait	buy	be	move	enjoy

1. We hoped it _____would be_____ sunny for our picnic.

2. I pushed the horse hard but it _____.

3. I asked Dad if he _____ me some ice cream.

4. _____ you _____ some more orange juice?

5. Sally switched on her computer but it _____.

6. Mom and Dad said they _____ me to the zoo as a treat.

7. We sat in the house and wished the rain _____.

8. Uncle David said he _____ me with my homework.

9. The man said he _____ until the doctor was free.

10. I knew you _____ playing my new video game.

Exercise 3

Tell whether each sentence below uses **may** or **may not** correctly. Show a correct use with a checkmark ✓ or an incorrect use with an x ☒ .

1. Andrew may not go out to play now because he has finished his homework.

2. Take an umbrella. It may not rain.

3. Please may we not watch television now?

4. You may not hurt yourself with that sharp knife.

5. I may come out to play later if I'm feeling better.

6. They are late. The bus may not have broken down.

7. "May I read the story you have written?" "Yes, you may not."

8. "May Andrew stay for dinner?" "Yes, he may."

Exercise 4

Complete the sentences using should or shouldn't and a verb from the list below. The first one has been done for you.

go	eat	stop	believe	think
wait	try	read	let	listen

1. They ___should stop___ making all that noise. It's disturbing people.

2. Mom says I _____ more vegetables.

3. We _____ everything we see on television.

4. You _____ more about other people and less about yourself.

5. It's getting late. I _____ home now.

6. You _____ your best.

7. You _____ letters that are addressed to other people.

8. Parents _____ their children go out after dark.

9. Students _____ outside the door until the teacher tells them to come in.

10. Children _____ to the advice their parents give them.

Exercise 5

Now rewrite the sentences from Exercise 4 above, using ought to or ought not to.

1. _____

_____

2. _____

_____

3. _____

_____

4. _____

_____

5. _____

_____

6. _____

_____

7. _____

_____

8. _____

_____

9. _____

_____

10. _____

_____

Exercise 6

Complete the sentences using must or mustn't with a verb from the list below. The first one has been done for you.

go	eat	stop	believe	tell
steal	be	read	park	listen

1. You _____*must stop*_____ at the curb and look before you cross the street.

2. Children _____ to the teacher if they want to learn.

3. You _____ everything your friends tell you.

4. You _____ the question carefully before you write the answer.

5. If you want to be healthy, you _____ a lot of fruits and vegetables.

6. You _____ out on your own at night.

7. We _____ because it is wrong.

8. Drivers _____ their cars in the middle of the road.

9. If you want people to be nice to you, you _____ nasty to them.

10. You _____ always _____ the truth.

7 Adverbs and Adverb Phrases

Adverbs are words that **tell you more about verbs, adjectives and other adverbs**. Many adverbs end in **ly**. You make these adverbs by adding **ly** to adjectives.

> She writes **neatly**.
>
> The traffic was moving **slowly**.
>
> We waited **patiently** to see the doctor.
>
> They waved goodbye **sadly**.
>
> David sings **beautifully**.
>
> The children walked **quickly** into the classroom.

Adverb phrases are groups of words that functions as single adverbs to describe the action of the verb.

> Are you sitting **in a comfortable chair**?
>
> Mr. Dickson always dresses **in fashionable clothes**.
>
> He draws cartoons **like a real cartoonist**.
>
> The train arrived **on time**.

Adverbs of Manner

Some adverbs and adverb phrases describe **the way** people do things. They answer the question "How?"

> The girls answered all the questions **correctly**.
>
> He was driving **carelessly**.
>
> The plane landed **safely**.
>
> Katy plays the piano **skillfully**.
>
> Sam is behaving **like a baby**.
>
> Please speak **in a clear voice**.
>
> She writes **in a very grown-up way**.
>
> You can buy fruit **very cheaply** in this shop.
>
> They sell everything **at very low prices**.
>
> David sings **like a professional singer**.

95

Adverbs of Time

Some adverbs and adverb phrases answer the question **"when?"** They are called **adverbs of time**.

I'm going to my new school **tomorrow**.

The train has **already** left.

We moved into our new house **last week**.

My big brother goes to college **in the autumn**.

Our favorite TV program starts **at 6 o'clock**.

It rained heavily **last night**.

We're going on a trip **in a few days' time**.

We'll leave **as soon as possible**.

My shoes will be too small for me **next year**.

I haven't seen Mom **this morning**. Is she working **today**?

Adverbs of Place

Some adverbs and adverb phrases answer the question **"where?"** They are called **adverbs of place**.

It's very sunny but cold **outside**.

The boys are playing **upstairs**.

That's our ball **there**.

I couldn't find my book **anywhere**.

They live in a house **nearby**.

The dog is **in the garden**.

Flowers like these grow **in the park**.

We're going **to New York City** on our school trip.

My brother is studying **at an English university**.

They live **on the northern side of the island**.

Adverbs of Frequency

Some adverbs and adverb phrases answer the question **"how often?"** They are called **adverbs of frequency**.

Katy practices the piano **regularly**.

The children **always** go to school on the bus.

I'll **never** make that mistake again.

Have you **ever** been to Japan?

We've been to Disneyland **twice**.

The shops are **often** very busy.

The newspaper is delivered **daily**.

We walk home from school **every day**.

I clean my bedroom **every week**.

Have you forgotten my name? I've told you **three times** already.

Dad polishes his shoes **twice a week**.

You should go to the dentist **once every six months**.

Adverbs of Duration

Some adverbs and adverb phrases answer the question **"how long?"** They are called **adverbs of duration**.

The library is **temporarily** closed.

We're staying in a hotel **overnight**.

The teacher left the classroom **briefly**.

The snow lasted **for three days**.

Mom was away **a very long time**.

Stand still **for a moment** while I comb your hair.

He talked to his girlfriend **for over an hour**.

We waited **for ages** for a bus.

I haven't seen my cousins **for two years**.

We stayed up **all night** talking.

The library is closed today and tomorrow (10 & 11 May). It will be reopened on 12 May.

Librarian

97

Adverbs of Emphasis

We have seen that most adverbs describe verbs, but remember that some adverbs also **describe adjectives or other adverbs**. They are usually used to **add emphasis**.

Here are some examples. The emphasizing adverbs are printed in bold. The adjectives or adverbs they describe are printed in color.

Anna can run **really** fast.

That's a **very** good drawing.

My rice is **too** hot.

The film was **just** terrible.

Your excuses are **completely** unbelievable.

These old tools are **totally** useless.

She sings **quite** beautifully.

Exercise 1

*Choose an adjective from the box and turn it into an **adverb** to complete the sentences below. The first one has been done for you.*

close	firm	bright	neat	careful
quick	sad	regular	quiet	clear

1. She writes very _____neatly_____.

2. You have to talk _____ when you're in the library.

3. Carry the glass _____ so you don't drop it.

4. You should exercise _____ if you want to stay fit.

5. "Goodbye. I'm going to miss you," she said _____ .

6. The sky was blue and the sun was shining _____ .

7. If you follow us _____ , you won't get lost.

8. I can't understand you. Please speak more _____ .

9. Let's walk _____ so we get home before it starts to rain.

10. Attach the sign _____ to the wall.

Exercise 2

*Are the bold words in the following sentences adverbs or adjectives? Write **adverb** or **adjective** on the line after each sentence.*

1. The teacher smiled **kindly**. _____

2. She has a **lovely** smile. _____

3. The children in my class are very **friendly**. _____

4. John had no friends and felt very **lonely**. _____

5. It was raining, so they **wisely** decided to stay in. _____

6. My dad buys a **daily** newspaper. _____

7. Some snakes are **deadly**. _____

8. I've **nearly** finished my homework. _____

9. I shook hands **politely** with the head teacher. _____

10. They played some very **lively** games. _____

Exercise 3

*Circle the verb in each sentence below. Then underline the **adverb** or **adverb phrase** that describes the verb. What kind of adverb is it? Write **M** for manner, **T** for time, **P** for place, **F** for frequency or **D** for duration in the box after each sentence. The first one has been done for you.*

1. Kent did his homework carelessly.	M
2. We start our vacation next week.	
3. Farah read the poem in a very clear voice.	
4. The accident happened during the afternoon.	
5. The man walked very slowly.	
6. My cousin arrived yesterday.	
7. I left my schoolbag in the car.	
8. It stopped raining for a few minutes.	
9. Dad goes jogging regularly.	
10. We eat our meals in the dining room.	

Complete the sentences with an **adverb** or **adverb phrase** from the box. The kind of adverb you will need is in parentheses after each sentence. The first one has been done for you.

outside	this morning	ever	on the bus	clearly
all day	in old clothes	for a week	already	every day

1. His face was dirty and he was dressed _____ in old clothes _____ . (**manner**)

2. Have you _____ been in a plane? (**frequency**)

3. She was so ill that she missed school _____ . (**duration**)

4. I did some homework last night and finished it _____ . (**time**)

5. We went _____ to play. (**place**)

6. Dad takes the dog for a walk _____ . (**frequency**)

7. Sally left her pencil case _____ . (**place**)

8. Speak _____ so everyone can hear you. (**manner**)

9. It was a fine day and the children played in the garden _____ . (**duration**)

10. "Go and do your homework." "I've _____ done it." (**time**)

8 Prepositions and Prepositional Phrases

Prepositions are words that show a connection between other words. Most prepositions are little words like **at**, **in** and **on**. Prepositional phrases are groups of words, such as **out of** and **on top of**.

Preposition or Adverb?

Some words can be used either as prepositions or as adverbs. If the word **is followed by a noun or a pronoun**, it is a **preposition**.

Look at these pairs of examples. In each of the sentences marked **preposition**, there is a noun or pronoun after the preposition. This noun or pronoun is called the **object of the preposition**. Notice that objects are printed in color.

She put her hand **inside** my **bag**.
                    ▲   ▲
               [preposition] [noun]

It was raining, so they decided to stay **inside**.
                                      ▲
                                  [adverb]

His friends walked **past** **him** without speaking.
                    ▲   ▲
               [preposition] [noun]

A car drove **past** at high speed.
                    ▲
               [adverb]

John's house is **across** the **street**.
                  ▲   ▲
             [preposition] [noun]

They got into the boat and rowed **across**.
                               ▲
                           [adverb]

Water was running **down** the **walls**.
                  ▲   ▲
             [preposition] [noun]

He tripped over his shoelaces and fell **down**.
                                    ▲
                                    [adverb]

Prepositions of Place

Some prepositions show **where** something happens. They are called **prepositions of place**.

Sally was sitting **under** a tree.

There's a wooden floor **underneath** the carpet.

Some geese flew **over** their house.

John and Sarah were hiding **inside** the wardrobe.

There was a tree **beside** the river.

I have a friend who lives **in** Wyoming.

A big truck parked **in front of** their car.

The cat jumped **on top of** the cupboard.

One girl sits **in the middle of** the playground and the others dance round her.

Prepositions of Time

Some prepositions show **when** something happens. They are called **prepositions of time**.

School starts **at** nine o'clock.

I brush my teeth **in** the morning and **at** night.

We're going to the zoo **on** Saturday.

No, you can't watch a video. It's **past** your bedtime already.

I visited my grandparents **during** the summer.

You must finish the work **by** Friday.

I'll do my homework **before** dinner.

"Mom, can you help me with my homework?" "Not now. You'll have to wait **until** this afternoon."

Prepositions of Direction

Some prepositions show **where** something is going. They are called **prepositions of direction**.

The boys chased **after** each other.

The football rolled **down** the hill.

A man was walking his dog **along** the riverbank.

The freeway goes right **through** the city.

We were travelling **towards** Miami.

A girl went **past** them on a bike.

This road leads **away from** the stadium.

They watched the train pull **out of** the station.

Prepositions with Special Uses

Many prepositions are used in other ways. Here are some of them.

of

I bought a bag **of** rice and a quart **of** milk.

Would you like a glass **of** orange juice?

Kathleen is a member **of** the chess club.

I need three pieces **of** paper.

Most **of** the children in my class like school.

There are several ways **of** cooking meat.

for

I made this bookmark **for** Mom.

Is there room **for** me on this seat?

I'd like a new computer **for** Christmas.

We're going downtown **for** a meeting.

What's this bag **for**?

This word is too difficult **for** me to spell.

with

He pounds nails in **with** a hammer.

Mix the flour **with** water.

She painted the picture **with** her new paints.

Would you like to come **with** us to the arcade?

I can do difficult problems **with** help from Mom.

Who is the man **with** the beard?

Michael came home **with** dirty hands.

Cross the busy street **with** care.

except and instead of

I like all kinds of food **except** pasta.

Everyone likes chocolate **except** Tom.

We go to school every day **except** Saturday and Sunday.

You should eat fruit **instead of** candy.

Dad is coming to the theater with us **instead of** Mom.

We could watch TV **instead of** reading our books.

like, as and than

The words **like, as** and **than** are used to compare things.

Kathleen looks **like** her dad.

Andrew smiles **like** his mother.

Peter sings **like** a professional singer.

Are these shoes the same **as** those?

Sue is nearly as tall **as** the teacher.

My backpack is bigger **than** John's.

Dad is taller **than** all of us.

This painting is more beautiful **than** that one.

The neighborhood streets are less busy **than** downtown streets.

Prepositions with Adjectives, Verbs or Nouns

▶ Prepositions are used with some **adjectives**. The adjectives in these examples are printed in color.

Dad was **angry** **with** us.

We were **afraid** **of** the big dog.

She's not very **interested** **in** sports.

John is very **good** **at** drawing.

Mr. Lee is **pleased** **with** our work.

The teachers are always **kind** **to** us.

What's **wrong** **with** the computer?

▶ Prepositions are used with some **verbs**. The verbs in these examples are printed in color.

I'm **looking** **for** my pencil. Have you seen it?

Can you **think** **of** another word for 'pleased'?

Does this book **belong** **to** you?

We're **listening** **to** CDs.

I **agree** **with** you.

I **lent** my skateboard **to** Sue.

Tell me **about** the show you saw.

Cut the cake **into** five pieces.

They **borrowed** money **from** the bank.

▶ Prepositions are used with some **nouns**. The nouns in these examples are printed in color.

What's the **answer** **to** this question?

Is there a **reason** **for** this delay?

What's the **matter** **with** you?

Here's an **example** **of** good behavior.

Congratulations **on** winning the competition!

Traffic can cause **damage** **to** the environment.

Exercise 1

Underline the **prepositions** *in the following sentences.*

1. There was a sign above the door.
2. The ball rolled under a car.
3. She put the letter in her pocket.
4. Sam hid behind the fence.
5. Tuesday comes after Monday.
6. Mr. Shin is from Korea.
7. The train went through the station without stopping.
8. I left the book on the table.
9. My favorite TV program starts at 6:00 o'clock.
10. There's a path between the two houses.

Exercise 2

Complete the following sentences with the **prepositions** *from the box. The type of preposition you need is in parentheses. The first sentence has been done for you.*

after	under	toward	during	on
in	before	at	away from	across

1. A cat was sitting _____on_____ the roof of my car. (**place**)
2. Some people were talking _____ the movie. (**time**)
3. A man was coming _____ us on his bike. (**direction**)
4. The party starts _____ six o'clock. (**time**)
5. She put the book _____ her bag. (**place**)
6. We walked _____ the street to the park. (**place**)
7. I'll be late for school! It's _____ nine o'clock already! (**time**)
8. She keeps her slippers _____ her bed. (**place**)
9. We always wash our hands _____ meals. (**time**)
10. She ran _____ the dog because she was frightened. (**direction**)

106

Exercise 3

Circle the preposition in each sentence. Then underline the noun or pronoun that is the object of the preposition. The first one has been done for you.

1. There is a new bookstore (across) the street.

2. Which letter comes after D?

3. She found the missing ticket under the carpet.

4. We opened the cupboard and found nothing in it.

5. Mom keeps a family photograph on her desk.

6. Students mustn't talk during the exam.

7. Our vacation starts on Friday.

8. You can play outside after lunch.

9. We ran inside the house when it started to rain.

10. A plane flew over their heads.

Exercise 4

Complete each sentence by using a preposition from the box.

of	for	with	except	instead of

1. We baked a cake _____ Mom's birthday.

2. All the boys went swimming _____ Tom.

3. Can I come _____ you to the beach?

4. Most _____ the children in my class like computer games.

5. Stir the sauce _____ a wooden spoon.

6. Would you like rice _____ pasta?

7. How many pounds _____ hamburger did you buy?

8. Dad is good at everything _____ cooking.

9. Children, what would you like _____ dinner?

10. Who's the lady _____ the long blonde hair?

Exercise 5

*Read the following sentences. Then tell whether **like**, **as** and **than** are used correctly in each sentence. Put a checkmark ☑ in the box for a correct use and put an x ☒ in the box for an incorrect use. If the wrong preposition is used, write the correct preposition on the line. The first one has been done for you.*

1. John is nearly as tall **than** his dad.   ✗   _____as_____

2. Our house is smaller **than** David's.   ☐   _____

3. That car isn't the same **like** this one.   ☐   _____

4. Sally plays tennis **like** a professional player.   ☐   _____

5. This video is longer **than** the one we watched last night.   ☐   _____

6. Whales look **as** dolphins but they're much bigger.   ☐   _____

7. The wind sometimes sounds **like** a howling dog.   ☐   _____

8. This ring is more expensive **as** that one.   ☐   _____

9. The sea was as calm **as** a swimming pool.   ☐   _____

10. Mom is a few months younger **than** Dad.   ☐   _____

9 Conjunctions

Conjunctions are words used to link words, phrases or clauses.
Some common conjunctions are **and**, **but** and **or**.

and, but *and* or

▶ Use **and** to link words that are **similar**.

> We buy fruit **and** vegetables at the grocery store.
>
> The president visited towns **and** cities across the country.
>
> The house is warm **and** comfortable.
>
> The weather was cold **and** windy.
>
> There were several cars **and** trucks in the street.

and

▶ Use **but** to link words that are **different** and do not normally go together.

> He works quickly **but** neatly.
>
> The teacher is firm **but** fair with the children.
>
> The musicians are young **but** very talented.
>
> The weather was sunny **but** cold.
>
> Karate is tiring **but** fun.
>
> We want a vacation that's interesting **but** relaxing.
>
> Some animals are big **but** gentle.

▶ Use **or** to talk about **choices**.

> You can have a soda **or** lemonade.
>
> Would you like pasta **or** rice?
>
> Who is cooking the dinner, Mom **or** Dad?
>
> Does the sauce taste sweet **or** sour?
>
> Do we turn right **or** left?
>
> Is your sister older **or** younger than you?
>
> Should the children bring bikes **or** skateboards?

or

▶ The word **or** is often used with **not** and other negative words.

> She does **not** like apple juice **or** orange juice.
>
> I did**n't** see **or** hear anything strange.
>
> He can**'t** sing **or** dance.
>
> They've **never** been to Europe **or** Asia.

Conjunctions Linking Phrases

Use the conjunctions **and**, **but** and **or** to link **phrases**. The phrases in these examples are printed in color.

> We like going shopping **and** visiting museums.
>
> I tell my parents **and** my best friend all my secrets.
>
> Some of my toys are dirty **and** a bit broken.
>
> The car is very old **but** still very reliable.
>
> The weather was very sunny **but** rather cold.
>
> I'm older than Anna **but** younger than Jack.
>
> Is it quicker to go by train **or** by car?
>
> You could call it a thin book **or** a thick magazine.
>
> She couldn't decide whether to stay in bed **or** get up and take a shower.

Conjunctions with Lists

Use the conjunctions **and** and **or** with lists of words. Remember to put a **comma** between the words. Then use **and** or **or** between the last two words.

> We bought milk, eggs, cheese **and** butter.
>
> My favorite teachers are Mr. Lee, Mrs. Carter **and** Mr. Park.
>
> In the morning I get up, take a shower, eat breakfast **and** brush my teeth.
>
> Kathleen didn't have any paper, pens **or** pencils.
>
> People travel to work by car, bus **or** train.
>
> I haven't eaten breakfast, lunch **or** dinner.

Conjunctions That Join Sentences

Conjunctions are also used **to join two sentences** to make them one.
Here are some examples with **and**, **but** and **or**.

Mom is working in the garden. Dad is busy in the kitchen.
Mom is working in the garden and Dad is busy in the kitchen.

Sam is playing football. Eric is reading a book.
Sam is playing football and Eric is reading a book.

I switched on the TV. There were no interesting programs on.
I switched on the TV, but there were no interesting programs on.

Meera phoned her friend Anna. She wasn't at home.
Meera phoned her friend Anna, but she wasn't at home.

Would you like to go to the movies? Shall we go
for a burger?
Would you like to go to the movies or shall we
go for a burger?

Hurry up! You'll be late for school.
Hurry up or you'll be late for school!

Notes

A long sentence with two parts that are linked by **and**, **but** or **or** is called a **compound sentence**.

Other Words for *and*

There are other words for **and** that also join two sentences.

Dad washed the car. He polished it.
Dad **not only** washed the car, **but he also** polished it.

Sally baked the cake. She decorated it.
Sally **not only** baked the cake, **but** she decorated it **as well**.

John did his homework. He cleaned his room.
John **not only** did his homework, **but** he cleaned his room, too.

They visited Sydney. They also visited Hong Kong and Tokyo.
They visited Sydney, **as well as** Hong Kong **and** Tokyo.

Sam ran faster than Kim. He ran faster than David too.
Sam ran faster than **both** Kim **and** David.

Other Words Used for *but*

There are other words for **but** that also join sentences.

Grandpa is old **but** very fit.
Although Grandpa is old, he's very fit.

The weather was sunny **but** cold.
Even though the weather was sunny, it was cold.

The bus is slower than the train **but** it's cheaper.
While the bus is slower than the train, it's cheaper.

This computer is very old **but** reliable.
Though this computer is very old, it is very reliable.

Other Words for *or*

There are other words for **or** that name choices or join two sentences.

The movie wasn't funny. It wasn't interesting.
The movie was **neither** funny **nor** interesting.

You can do your homework now. You can do your homework after dinner.
You can do your homework **either** now **or** after dinner.

We could walk. We could take a taxi.
We could walk, **or else** take a taxi.

Conjunctions of Time

The conjunctions **before**, **after**, **since**, **until**, **when**, **while**, **as** and **as soon as** are used to say when something happens. They are called **conjunctions of time**.

Take the toy out of the box **before** you throw the box away.

Before you leave the house, be sure that you've got your backpack.

I usually do my homework **after** I have my dinner.

After I went to bed, I heard a strange noise downstairs.

We've moved to a new house **since** I last wrote to you.

Since the new teacher arrived, we all enjoy our work more.

You can't watch TV **until** you've done your homework.

Until the rice is cooked, we can't eat dinner.

I'll call you **when** I get home.

When the wind blows, the branches on the tree bend.

Dad watches TV **while** he does his exercises.

While we're waiting for the bus, let's play a game.

People stand back **as** the train goes through the station.

As the president's car goes past, everybody waves.

We went inside **as soon as** it started to rain.

As soon as you've finished your homework, let me see it.

Conjunctions of Place

The conjunctions **where** and **wherever** are used to talk about places. They are called **conjunctions of place**.

Does anybody know **where** Mr. Carter lives?

Where the road is narrow, big trucks can't get through.

The dog follows Andrew **wherever** he goes.

Wherever there are mountains, you will also find streams.

Conjunctions of Reason

The conjunctions **because**, **since**, **as** and **in case** tell why someone does something. They are called **conjunctions of reason**.

I sat down **because** I was feeling tired.

Because we arrived late, we missed the beginning of the play.

I took an apple **since** it was the only fruit in the bowl.

Since you have finished your homework, you can help me make dinner.

Mom switched off the TV **as** it was past my bedtime.

As you're my best friend, I'll lend you my new bike.

Take an umbrella **in case** it rains.

In case you forget the number, I've written it on this piece of paper.

Conjunctions of Purpose

The conjunctions **so**, **so that** and **in order to** tell what the purpose of something is. They are called **conjunctions of purpose**.

The children are wearing hats **so** they won't get sunburned.

John finished his homework before dinner **so** he could watch his favorite TV program.

Let's write down the address **so** we don't forget it.

We left early **so that** we wouldn't be late.

John took a map **so that** he wouldn't get lost.

I hid the comics under the bed **so that** nobody could find them.

She goes jogging every morning **in order to** keep fit.

In order to get to sleep, he reads a really boring book at bedtime.

Dad painted the walls white **in order to** make the room look brighter.

Exercise 1

Complete the following sentences by adding and, but or or.

1. Mrs. Taylor is tall _____ slim.

2. Learning geography is hard _____ interesting.

3. I don't like football _____ soccer.

4. Do you pull the handle _____ push it?

5. These tools are old _____ still useful.

6. We visited lots of castles _____ palaces in England.

7. The classes are quite difficult _____ I'm doing well.

8. I didn't know whether to turn left _____ right.

Exercise 2

Complete the following sentences by adding commas and and or or. The first one has been done for you.

1. You'll need paper scissors glue.

   You'll need paper, scissors and glue. _____.

2. I don't enjoy football swimming homework.

   _____.

3. Shall we play tennis read a book watch TV?

   _____.

4. Do you want to sit next to Peter David Sam?

   _____.

5. We visited India Japan South Korea on our trip.

   _____.

6. Mr. Carter likes classical music pop music jazz.

   _____.

7. No one likes people who are rude mean cruel.

   _____.

8. Dad has to make our breakfast help us get dressed take us to school.

   _____.

Choose the sentence from the box that goes with each sentence below. Join the two sentences with **and, but** or **or**. The first one has been done for you.

> You weren't at home.
> Draw a picture of your favorite animal.
> Nobody answered.
> Do you want to play at my house?
> It was closed.
>
> Put it in the fridge.
> We couldn't find it.
> Will he drop it?
> Is Nicole smarter?
> She didn't know the answer.

1. Shall I bring my computer games to your house?

   <u>Shall I bring my computer games to your house or do you want to play at my house?</u>

2. We went to the supermarket.

   _____.

3. Take this milk.

   _____.

4. We looked everywhere for the key.

   _____.

5. I phoned you this morning.

   _____.

6. Jim asked the teacher.

   _____.

7. Take a pencil.

   _____.

8. Is Susan the smartest student in the class?

   _____.

9. Do you think he'll catch the ball?

   _____.

10. We knocked at the door.

    _____.

Complete each sentence with one of the sentence parts in the box. Underline the
conjunction in your sentence. The first one has been done for you.

> in case the ground is muddy.
>
> as soon as you've done your homework.
>
> where I had spilled the juice.
>
> so he could show it to his friends.
>
> because it had started to rain.
>
> so you're not tired in the morning.
>
> before you start to paint.
>
> since I last saw my cousin.
>
> until it is soft enough to eat.
>
> while their dad cooked dinner.

1. The children went inside

   The children went inside <u>because</u> it had started to rain.

2. He took his new toy to school

   _____.

3. Put on your apron

   _____.

4. The children played in the garden

   _____.

5. Wear your boots

   _____.

6. You can watch a video

   _____.

7. There was a mark on the carpet

   _____.

8. Cook the pasta

   _____.

9. Go to bed early

   _____.

10. It's been six months

    _____.

10 Sentences

A **sentence** is a group of words that expresses a complete thought. Sentences always have a **subject** and a **verb**.

subject	verb
She	is working.
He	is reading.
The children	are playing.
They	are singing.

Four Kinds of Sentence

A **declarative sentence** makes a **statement**.

> It is raining.
> Tom likes football.
> The school bell was ringing.
> The children are playing with the dog.
> Topeka is in Kansas.

Notes

A declarative sentence ends with a **period**.

An **interrogative sentence** asks a **question**.

> Where are my keys?
> Why is the sky blue?
> Who is talking to the teacher?
> Is this the way to the ice skating rink?

Notes

An interrogative sentence ends with a **question mark** (?) instead of a period.

An **exclamatory sentence** makes a very strong statement called an **exclamation**. It shows a strong feeling such as surprise or anger.

> What a kind thing to do!
> How beautiful she is!
> The silly boy!

Notes

An exclamatory sentence ends with an **exclamation point** (!) instead of a period.

118

An **imperative sentence** gives an **order**.

Ask Tom to come and see me.

Don't tell me lies.

Please leave.

Go to your room!

Speak up!

N o t e s

An imperative sentence can end with an **exclamation point (!)** if the order is very firm.

Sentences with Objects

The **subject** of a sentence often does something to another person or thing. The person or thing that receives the action of the subject is called the **object** of the verb. Verbs that have objects are called **transitive verbs**.

Here are some sentences with transitive verbs.

subject	transitive verb	object
Dad	is reading	a book.
I	am cooking	dinner.
You	have broken	my new toy.
Mom	likes	her new car.
She	has forgotten	her backpack.
The dog	licked	my face.
Our ball	hit	a window.
They	visited	the museum.
Anna	is sewing	a dress for her doll.
Uncle Ben	sent	a package to his friend.

Verbs with Two Objects

Some verbs have two objects. Look at the sentence below.

Sam **gave** Anna a present.

indirect object   direct object

The thing that Sam gives is 'a present', so **a present** is the **direct object** of the verb. But there is another object: 'Anna'. 'Anna' is the person that receives the present, so **Anna** is the **indirect object** of the verb. Many verbs have both direct and indirect objects. Here are some examples.

subject	verb	indirect object	direct object
Dad	is reading	the children	a story.
Grandma	is baking	me	a cake.
A kind man	showed	us	the way.
We	have brought	you	some new magazines to read.
Mr. Berg	is teaching	the children	French.
Jack	asked	the teacher	a question.
I	am writing	my friend	a letter.
She	sent	her cousin	an email.
John	has found	us	a secret place to play.
Uncle Andy	told	them	the good news.

Verbs with No Object

Some verbs don't have an object. A verb that does not have an object is called an **intransitive verb**. Here are some sentences with intransitive verbs.

Mr. Park usually **walks** to work.

The sun **is shining**.

I don't **know**.

The man **smiled**.

Miss Lee always **dresses** very smartly.

Anna **talks** a lot in class.

It **is snowing**.

We **have** already **eaten**.

Dad always **drives** carefully.

Can your little brother **read**?

Tell whether each sentence below is a **declarative sentence**, an **interrogative sentence**, an **exclamatory sentence** or an **imperative sentence**.
The first one has been done for you.

1. The girls were playing volleyball.   declarative sentence

2. Where is my bike? _____

3. What a lovely dog! _____

4. It's snowing again today. _____

5. Please show me that pair of black shoes. _____

6. Can Anna come out to play? _____

7. Do your homework now. _____

8. What time is it? _____

9. Pass me the orange juice, please. _____

10. On weekends, I often go fishing with Dad. _____

11. Can your little brother read? _____

12. Speak in a loud, clear voice. _____

13. That was a fantastic game! _____

14. What fun this is! _____

15. Jamal really likes horses. _____

Exercise 2

Underline the verbs in these sentences. Then tell whether each verb is **transitive** or **intransitive**. Put a checkmark in the correct box.

	transitive verb	intransitive verb
1. Dad is baking bread.		
2. We buy our food at the supermarket.		
3. We are learning Latin.		
4. Come with me now.		
5. The children went to bed.		

Exercise 3

Underline the objects in the following sentences. Write **D** for **direct object** or **I** for **indirect object** above each one. The first one has been done for you.

1. Uncle Bill gave Michael some money.

 (I above "Michael", D above "some money")

2. Mom is baking us a chocolate cake for Christmas.

3. The children crossed the road safely.

4. Please pass me that pencil.

5. Henry sent Sam a letter from Japan.

6. I've forgotten your name.

7. She's always giving her students advice.

8. We gave Dad a watch for his birthday.

Exercise 4

All the following sentences have **verbs with direct objects.** Rewrite each sentence, adding an **indirect object** to it. For example, for the first sentence you could write:

   Dad bought Mom some flowers.

1. Dad bought some flowers.

   _____

2. The teacher found an empty seat.

   _____

3. The police officer showed her badge.

   _____

4. Rudy sent a postcard.

   _____

5. Will you buy some bread at the supermarket ?

   _____

6. I'll bring my stamp collection.

   _____

Simple Sentences

A **clause** is a group of words that contains **one subject** and **one verb**. A sentence that consists of one clause is called a **simple sentence**. Here are some examples. The subjects are printed in bold and the verbs are printed in color.

The girls are playing baseball.

Sally found a good hiding place.

I am eating my breakfast.

Tom is wearing his new shoes today.

Will **you** help me?

The sky was very cloudy.

I can hear the birds.

Everyone was happy.

Is **it** raining again?

Compound Sentences

A **compound sentence** contains **two clauses** joined by a conjunction such as **and**, **or**, **but** or **so**. Look at these examples. The verbs in the clauses are printed in color. Notice that there are **two verbs**, one on each side of the conjunction.

Some people are always happy **and** some people are always sad.
She opened the bag **and** took out a book.

Do you want coffee **or** would you prefer lemonade?
Is that a bird **or** is it a plane?

John is good at English **but** he's not very good at math.
Michael wants to see Star Wars **but** his friends have already seen it.

Tom dropped his sandwich **so** I gave him mine.
It started to rain **so** we went inside.

Conditional Sentences

▶ To talk about things that are possible, you often use **if** in a sentence. A sentence with **if** is called a **conditional sentence**. Here is an example of a conditional sentence with the **if-clause** printed in color.

If it **rains** tomorrow, we **shall** not **go** to the beach.

simple present tense verb	shall/will + infinitive

In the **if-clause**, use a **verb** in the simple present tense. In the **main clause**, use **shall** or **will** and **an infinitive**. Here are some more examples. The if-clauses are in color and the main clauses are in bold print.

If there**'s** no rice in the cupboard, we**'ll buy** some more.

If we **don't work** hard, we**'ll** never **learn**.

If we **leave** now, we**'ll arrive** on time.

▶ You may also put the main clause **before** the if-clause.

We**'ll play** indoors if it **rains**.

You**'ll get** sick if you **don't eat** good food.

Sam **will do** well in his piano recital if he **practices** regularly.

Positive and Negative Sentences

▶ A **positive sentence** tells you about something that exists or something that is happening.

I like ice cream.

Michael is my brother.

The train leaves at five o'clock.

I'm feeling really tired.

She's finished her homework.

Dad is in the kitchen.

There's a cartoon on TV.

A **negative sentence** contains the word **not** or another **negative word**. Negative sentences tell you that something does not exist or is not happening. Here are some examples. The negative words are printed in bold.

I'm **not** very good at math.

Tom **isn't** as tall as Alan.

We **didn't** hear you shout at us.

Meera **hasn't** read the Harry Potter books.

People **can't** see very well in the dark.

There's **nothing** interesting on TV tonight.

We've **never** been to China or Japan.

Nobody knows my secret.

There are **no** coins in my pocket.

Exercise 5

*Are the following sentences **simple sentences** or **compound sentences**? Put a checkmark (✓) in the correct box. For each compound sentence you marked, write the conjunction in the blank space next to it. The first one has been done for you.*

	simple sentence	compound sentence	
1. The sun is shining and the sky is blue.		✓	and
2. Mom doesn't like spiders.			
3. Eat plenty of fruit and vegetables.			
4. Would you like rice or do you prefer pasta?			
5. Is your bag red or green?			
6. Sam saw me and he waved.			
7. Pass me the dictionary, please.			
8. I've never been to Ohio or Indiana.			
9. Our new teacher is a young man.			
10. Switch off the light and go to sleep.			

Match the **if-clauses** in the box with the **main clauses** below. Write two sentences for each pair of clauses. The first one has already been done for you.

if they get no water	if you don't write neatly
if we all work together	if we don't leave now
if you let me explain	if I need help
if you don't want to see this movie	if you work hard

1. you'll do well in your exams

   If you work hard, you'll do well in your exams.

   You'll do well in your exams if you work hard.

2. we'll be late

   _____

   _____

3. I won't be able to read your story

   _____

   _____

4. we'll choose a different movie

   _____

   _____

5. the plants will die

   _____

   _____

6. we'll finish the job more quickly

   _____

   _____

7. I'll tell you what happened

_____

_____

8. I'll ask Mom and Dad

_____

_____

_____

Exercise 7

Rewrite the following sentences to make them negative. Use negative words such as **no, not** *and* **never.** *Use contractions in some of your sentences. The first one has been done for you.*

1. Children like chocolate.

   Children don't like chocolate. _____

2. John is my best friend.

   _____

3. I've got a new bike.

   _____

4. Everybody knows where I live.

   _____

5. There's some food in the refrigerator.

   _____

6. I saw the boy throw the stone.

   _____

7. We want to go to the ballgame.

   _____

8. Sam always tells the truth.

   _____

Questions

There are two kinds of questions: **yes or no questions** and **question-word questions**.

▶ yes or no questions

When you ask a yes or no question, you want the answer **yes** or the answer **no**. Use the verbs **be**, **have** and **do** along with helping **verbs** such as **can**, **will** and **should** when you ask these questions. Here are some examples of yes or no questions, with answers.

Is this your seat?
Yes.

May I sit here?
Yes.

Can you ride a bike?
No.

Don't you like pizza?
No.

Do you like swimming?
Yes.

Are we late?
No.

▶ In questions, the **helping verb** comes **before** the subject. The **other verb** comes **after** the subject. The verb **be** also comes **before** the subject when it is an ordinary verb rather than a helping verb.

Here are some examples of statements and the questions you can make from them. Notice that the helping verbs are printed in bold and the subjects are in color.

statement	question
Dad is ill today.	**Is** Dad ill today?
She has finished her homework.	**Has** she finished her homework?
The cat doesn't like noise.	**Doesn't** the cat like noise?
Michael can ride a bike.	**Can** Michael ride a bike?
Sally could borrow your pencil.	**Could** Sally borrow your pencil?
You may leave now.	**May** I leave now?
I think it will rain tomorrow.	**Do** you think it will rain tomorrow?
I saw Tom at the football game.	**Did** you see Tom at the football game?
Miss Lee sang a song.	**Did** Miss Lee sing a song?
The computer needs to be repaired.	**Does** the computer need to be repaired?

Question-word questions

Use the question words **what**, **which**, **who** (sometimes **whom**), **whose**, **when**, **where** and **how** to ask for information. The verbs **be**, **have** and **do**, and **helping verbs** such as **can**, **will** and **should** are also used in questions.

The **helping verb** comes **before** the subject, as it does in yes or no questions. Here are some examples. Again, the helping verb is printed in bold and the subject is printed in color.

What **is your name**?

What date **is it** today?

Which boy **is your brother**?

Which house **do you** live in?

Who **is the boy** next to Alan?

Who (*or* Whom) **did he** ask?

Whose book **is this**?

When **can I** come to visit you?

When **does the spring vacation** start?

Where **is the pencil** that I left on my desk?

Where **do the birds** go when they fly away in winter?

How **can Grandma** read without her glasses?

How **does a plane** stay in the sky?

Sometimes the **wh-word** itself is the subject of the sentence. In this case, don't use **do** to form questions.

Who wants to come with me?

What caused the accident?

Which is the fastest car?

I've got my coat. **Whose** is this?

Question Tags

▶ Sometimes people finish what they are saying with a short question. Why do they do this? Because they want to know if the person they are speaking to agrees with them. This short question is called a **question tag**. Look at the following sentence.

> The weather is lovely today, **isn't it**?

The main part of the sentence is positive, but the **question tag** is negative. You expect the answer to a **negative question tag** to be **yes**. For example:

> "The weather is lovely today, **isn't it**?" "**Yes**, it is."

▶ Use a helping verb and the subject of the sentence to make the **question tag**. Notice that the subject has been replaced by a pronoun in the example sentences. The pronoun in the question tag refers to the subject printed in color.

> Tom is older than you, **isn't he**?
>
> Sally has got a dog, **hasn't she**?
>
> Anna and I can go by train, **can't we**?
>
> Peter and David should leave now, **shouldn't they**?

▶ If the main part of the sentence has **I am** in it, use **aren't I** in the question tag.

> I'm your best friend, **aren't I**?
>
> I'm taller than Sumiko, **aren't I**?

▶ If the main part of the sentence is negative, the **question tag** is positive. You expect the answer to **a positive question tag** to be **no**.

> These questions aren't very difficult, **are they**?
>
> You haven't read this book, **have you**?
>
> Peter isn't as tall as I am, **is he**?
>
> She isn't eight yet, **is she**?
>
> There aren't many clouds in the sky, **are there**?
>
> There isn't much wind today, **is there**?
>
> There weren't any emails for me, **were there**?

Exercise 8

Rewrite the following statements as *yes* or *no* questions. The first one has already been done for you.

1. It is raining again.

   <u>Is it raining again?</u>

2. She can speak Japanese.

   _____

3. Margaret is at home.

   _____

4. My mom works in an office.

   _____

5. The teacher told the children a story.

   _____

6. Philip has got a new bike.

   _____

7. She is Sumiko's best friend.

   _____

8. Tom could sit with David.

   _____

9. Dad will help Jennifer with her homework.

   _____

10. We will be late.

    _____

Choose one of the question words from the box to complete the sentences below.
You may use some of the words more than once. The first one has been done for you.

what	who	when	why
which	whose	where	how

1. __Where__ are my keys?

2. _____ is the tall boy at the back of the class?

3. _____ time did they arrive?

4. _____ is the problem?

5. "_____ are we going to the zoo?" "Tomorrow."

6. _____ do you know the answer?

7. _____ do the stars twinkle?

8. _____ coat is this?

9. _____ would you like for dinner?

10. _____ did you open the door without a key?

11. _____ is your favorite singer?

12. _____ does this train leave?

13. _____ bike is that over there?

14. _____ cafe do you prefer?

15. _____ can we find a restaurant?

Complete the following sentences by adding a question tag. Remember that a positive sentence needs a **negative question tag**, and a negative sentence needs a **positive question tag**. The first one has been done for you.

1. This is your house, ____isn't it____ ?

2. That isn't the right answer, _____ ?

3. Your sister is very pretty, _____ ?

4. Andrew can't ride a bike, _____ ?

5. You've already seen that movie, _____ ?

6. I'm lucky to have a friend like Alice, _____ ?

7. The tunnel was very dark, _____ ?

8. They didn't play very well, _____ ?

9. We shouldn't look at the answers first, _____ ?

10. Aunt Sarah could come to our house for dinner, _____ ?

11. There was a bag in the car, _____ ?

12. Sally hasn't got a dog, _____ ?

13. We mustn't be late, _____ ?

14. There is a post office nearby, _____ ?

15. There were some people in the park, _____ ?

16. We can stay an extra day, _____ ?

17. The journey won't take long, _____ ?

18. I'm your best friend, _____ ?

19. Andrew and Susan are your neighbors, _____ ?

20. You didn't see the dog in the garden, _____ ?

Direct Speech

The exact words that someone says are called **direct speech**. Quotation marks " " are used to set off direct speech.

> Mom said, "Where are my keys?"
>
> "This ice cream is delicious," said Tom.
>
> "Have you boys washed your hands?" asked Dad.
>
> "Please get out of the car," the police officer ordered.
>
> "What a beautiful dress!" said Sally.

Indirect Speech

You can report what someone says without using their exact words. To do this, use a verb like **say**, **ask** or **tell**, followed by **that**. This is called **indirect speech**. There are several differences between a sentence with direct speech and a sentence with indirect speech.

- You **don't use quotation marks** with indirect speech.
- You **change the tense of the verb**.
- You **change the pronouns and determiners**.

Here are some examples. The verb tenses that change are printed in bold and the pronouns and determiners that change are printed in color. Remember that the past tense of **can** is **could** and the past tense of **will** is **would**.

direct speech	indirect speech
Maggie said, "I **feel** ill."	Maggie said that she **felt** ill.
Sumiko said, "It**'s** time to leave."	Sumiko said that it **was** time to leave.
"I **can't** find my book," said Alice.	Alice said that she **couldn't** find her book.
"John **is hitting** me," said Peter.	Peter said that John **was hitting** him.
Dad said, "I **haven't had** my breakfast yet."	Dad said that he **hadn't had** his breakfast yet.
"My car **won't start**," said Mom.	Mom said that her car **wouldn't start**.

▶ In indirect speech people often leave out the conjunction **that**.

Maggie said ~~that~~ she felt ill.

Sumiko said ~~that~~ it was time to leave.

Alice said ~~that~~ she couldn't find her book.

Peter said ~~that~~ John was hitting him.

Dad said ~~that~~ he hadn't had his breakfast yet.

▶ When you are using indirect speech to report **a statement that is still true now**, you don't change the tense of the verb.

direct speech	indirect speech
John **said**, "My mom **doesn't like** fish."	John **said** that his mom **doesn't like** fish.
"I **live** in a house by the sea," **said** Anna.	Anna **said** that she **lives** in a house by the sea.
Dad **said**, "Paris **is** a beautiful city."	Dad **said** Paris **is** a beautiful city.

Indirect Commands

▶ Use verbs like **order**, **tell** and **warn** to report orders and instructions. The construction **to + verb** or **not to + verb** may also be used.

direct speech	indirect speech
The teacher said, "Stop running in the corridor!"	The teacher **ordered** us **to stop** running in the corridor.
"Put your books away, children," said Mr. Park.	Mr. Park **told** the children **to put** their books away.
Dad said to David, "Please help me by washing the dishes."	Dad **asked** David **to help** him by washing the dishes.
Jack said to Maggie, "Please don't tell anyone my secret!"	Jack **begged** Maggie **not to tell** anyone his secret.
Miss Lee said to Alan, "Don't be late again tomorrow."	Miss Lee **warned** Alan **not to be** late again the next day.

Indirect Questions

▶ The verb **ask** is usually used to report questions.

direct speech	indirect speech
Sally said, "Where is my backpack?"	Sally **asked** where her backpack was.
Peter said, "Have you finished your homework?"	Peter **asked** if I had finished my homework.

▶ To report a question, put the subject **before** the verb or helping verb. Remember that the subject comes **after** the helping verb when you ask a question. Here are some examples. The subjects are printed in bold and the verbs are printed in color.

asking a question	reporting a question
"Where are **they** going?"	I asked where **they** were going.
"Can **Jack** ride his bike?"	I asked if **Jack** could ride his bike.
"Did **Miss Lee** sing a song?"	I asked whether **Miss Lee** sang a song.
"Has **she** finished her homework?"	I asked if **she** had finished her homework.

▶ To report a **question-word question**, use the same **question word** in direct speech.

direct speech	indirect speech
Mom said, "**Where** are your shoes?"	Mom asked where my shoes were.
Maggie said, "**Who** has taken my pen?"	Maggie asked **who** had taken her pen.
"**What** time does the show start?" asked Sue.	Sue asked **what** time the show started.
Peter said, "**Why** did you leave before the end of the movie?"	Peter asked **why** I left before the end of the movie.

When you are reporting **yes or no questions**, use **if** or **whether** after the verb.

direct speech	indirect speech
"Is it raining?" asked Tom.	Tom asked **if** it was raining.
Alice said, "Can you help us?"	Alice asked **whether** I could help them.
Dad said, "Is the train on time?"	Dad asked **if** the train was on time.

Exercise 1

*Fill in the blank spaces with a **verb** in the correct tense. The first one has been done for you.*

direct speech	indirect speech
1. "I am very tired," said Dad.	Dad said that he ____was____ very tired.
2. "You look very handsome, Mike," said Mom.	Mom told Mike that he _____ very handsome.
3. The teacher said, "Sam has not made any mistakes."	The teacher said that Sam _____ not made any mistakes.
4. "I am losing my patience," said Mr. Carter.	Mr. Carter said that he _____ losing his patience.
5. "You can come to my house for dinner," Maggie told Jason.	Maggie told Jason that he _____ come to her house for dinner.
6. Dad said, "Hurry up or we will be late."	Dad told us to hurry up or we _____ be late.
7. "The train is coming," said Peter.	Peter said that the train _____ coming.
8. "I have cleaned up my room," said Kathleen.	Kathleen said that she _____ cleaned up her room.
9. The teacher said, "It is time to stop writing."	The teacher said that it _____ time to stop writing.
10. "I don't want to watch TV," said John.	John said that he _____ want to watch TV.

Complete these indirect speech sentences with the correct **pronoun** or **determiner**.
The first one has been done for you.

direct speech	indirect Speech
1. "My head is aching," said Sarah.	Sarah said that _____her_____ head was aching.
2. "I like your new bike,' Dan told me.	Dan told me that he liked _____ new bike.
3. Tom and Peter said, "We'll give you our seats."	Tom and Peter said that they would give us _____ seats.
4. "You can borrow my book," Michael said.	Michael said that I could borrow _____ book.
5. "I haven't brushed my teeth," said Paul.	Paul said that he hadn't brushed _____ teeth.
6. "You are late again," Mr. Chen told me.	Mr. Chen said that _____ was late again.
7. "We have finished our homework," said the boys.	The boys said that they had finished _____ homework.
8. Sue and Maggie said, "We want to watch football on TV."	Sue and Maggie said that _____ wanted to watch football on TV.
9. "I don't like your green hair," said Uncle David.	Uncle David said that _____ didn't like my green hair.
10. Dad said, "We'll have to phone for a taxi."	Dad said that _____ would have to phone for a taxi.

Rewrite the following sentences as *indirect questions* or *indirect commands*. The first one has been done for you.

1. "Are you feeling ill?" Mom asked.

    Mom asked if I was feeling ill.

2. "When will you finish the work?" Dad asked the plumber.

    _____

3. The teacher said, "Open your books, children."

    _____

4. "Turn the music down, Maggie," said Mom.

    _____

5. "Please take your shoes off at the door, Tom," said Uncle David.

    _____

6. "Have you read the Harry Potter books?" Michael asked.

    _____

7. Jenny said, "Would you like some more orange juice, Peter?"

    _____

8. "Don't be rude to your teacher, children," said the principal.

    _____

9. "Write your name at the top of the page, everyone," said Miss Lee.

    _____

10. "Does the ball belong to you boys?" the woman asked.

    _____

12 Punctuation

Punctuation Marks

Punctuation marks are signs such as periods, commas and question marks. They are used in sentences to make the meaning clear.

period ▪

▶ Put a period **at the end of a sentence.**

Tim lent me his skateboard.

The children are playing in the garden.

The train arrived late.

It's not a very sunny day.

comma ,

▶ Put a comma **between items in a list.**

You need paper, scissors and glue.

She likes reading, swimming, playing basketball and going to the movies.

Tom, May Ling, Sue and Christopher all went shopping together.

▶ Put a comma **after yes** and **no.**

"Do you like football?" "Yes, I like it very much."

"Is this your house?" "Yes, it is."

"Is it still snowing?" "No, it's stopped."

"Has Sarah had breakfast yet?" "No, she hasn't."

▶ You also put a comma **before or after the name of the person you are speaking to.**

Hello, Mr. Carter.

Miss Lee, can I borrow a pencil, please?

Goodbye, Andrew.

Commas are used **before** please **and** thank you.

Could you pass me that pencil, please?
"Would you like some more orange juice, David?" "Yes, please."
I've had enough to eat, thank you.
"Would you like another cupcake, Sally?" "No, thank you."

A comma is also used **between the parts of a place name.**

Chicago, Illinois
Tower Bridge, London
Athens, Georgia
the Lincoln Memorial, Washington DC

question mark ?

Write a question mark **at the end of a question**, instead of a period.

Can you hear me, children?   Didn't you read the sign?
Who is that man talking to Dad?   Where is my schoolbag?
Is there someone knocking at the door?   How many apples are left?

exclamation point !

Use an exclamation point at the end of a sentence that shows **a strong feeling** such as surprise or fear. An exclamation point is used instead of a period.

What a silly thing to do!   Help! A monster!
You're completely wrong!   What a shame!
I told you not to go out on your own!   How sad!

You can also use exclamation points with strong **orders**.

Sit down!   Don't touch that knife!
Be quiet!   Give me that ball!
Leave that computer alone!   Do it now!

Exclamation points are usually used after **interjections**.

People often use just one or two words to express a sudden feeling such as **fear**, **happiness**, **surprise** or **anger**, or in greeting somebody. These short expressions are called **interjections**. Here are some examples:

Hello**!**	Ouch**!**
Good morning**!**	Hurray**!**
Good night**!**	Help**!**
Well done**!**	Look out**!**
Oh dear**!**	Happy Birthday**!**

apostrophe `,`

Use an apostrophe with s to show **who something belongs to.**

This is Michael**'s** room.

This is my Dad**'s** desk.

Are you Kathleen**'s** mom?

This dog**'s** tail is very long.

The teacher collects everyone**'s** books at the end of the class.

Jack is going to his friend**'s** house for lunch.

You also use an apostrophe to show **where one or more letters are missing in a contraction.**

I**'m** (= am) the boy who lives next door.

She**'s** (= is) my best friend.

He**'s** (= has) been to Europe twice.

We**'re** (= are) going to the zoo today.

You**'re** (= are) my favorite uncle.

I**'d** (= had) better go home now.

You**'ve** (= have) got dirt on your new shoes.

He**'ll** (= will) lend you his bike.

quotation marks " "

▶ Use quotation marks around **the exact words that someone says**. You put the mark " at the beginning of the words, and the mark " at the end.

Use a **comma** before the last quotation mark, to separate the words from the rest of the sentence.

"This bike is mine," said Susan.

"I would like some apple juice, please," said the little boy.

"Let's play computer games," said James.

Suppose the exact words that someone says come after the rest of the sentence. In this case put a **period** before the last quotation mark.

Dad said, "Come inside and have lunch."

"John," said Mom, "please turn your music down."

▶ Put question marks and exclamation points in the same place as periods, **before the last quotation mark**.

"Is this the way to the station?" the man asked.

Sam said, "Can I borrow your pencil?"

"Don't do that!" said Mom.

John said, "What a great movie!"

colon :

▶ When you are reading a playscript, notice the colon **between the name of a character and the words that they speak**.

Jack: What have you got in the bag?

Maggie: My swimming suit.

Jack: When are you going swimming?

Maggie: This afternoon. Would you like to come?

Capital Letter

▶ Use a capital letter as the first letter of the **first word in a sentence**.

   Dogs have wet noses.

   Where is my ball?

   That isn't fair!

   This is my brother.

   You need a racket if you're going to play tennis.

▶ You also use a capital letter for the first letter of the **first word in direct speech**.

   Sam said, "**T**his is my brother."

   "**W**here is my ball?" Tom asked.

   Alice shouted, "**T**hat isn't fair!"

   "**Y**ou'll need a racket if you're going to play tennis," said Dad.

▶ The word **I** is always written as a capital letter.

   I'm really pleased with your work.

   Do you know what **I** got for my birthday?

   Paul and **I** asked if we could help.

▶ Use a capital letter to begin the **names of people and places**.

John	**A**ustralia	the **S**phinx
May **L**ing	**G**ermany	the **T**aj **M**ahal
David **B**eckham	the **U**nited **S**tates of **A**merica	the **G**rand **C**anyon
Dr. **R**aj	**M**exico **C**ity	the **G**reat **W**all of **C**hina
Miss **L**ee	**B**eijing	the **P**acific **O**cean
Grandad	**B**uckingham **P**alace	**M**ount **F**uji
Uncle **D**avid	the **S**tatue of **L**iberty	the **R**io **G**rande
Professor **P**ark	the **E**rie **C**anal	the **H**imalayas

▶ You also use capital letters after the **initials** in someone's name.

T.K. Lee
J.K. Rowling
J.R.R. Tolkien
M.C. Hammer

▶ The **days** of the week and **months** of the year begin with a capital letter.

Monday	January	July
Tuesday	February	August
Wednesday	March	September
Thursday	April	October
Friday	May	November
Saturday	June	December
Sunday		

▶ The names of **holidays** and **special celebrations** also begin with a capital letter.

Valentine's Day	Veterans' Day
Yom Kippur	Halloween
Christmas	Independence Day
Memorial Day	Thanksgiving

▶ Capital letters are also used in the **titles of books, films and plays**.

The Lady and the Tramp
Star Wars
Harry Potter and the Sorcerer's Stone
The Adventures of Sherlock Holmes
Alice in Wonderland
The Sword in the Stone
Hamlet, Prince of Denmark
Cats and Dogs
Universal World Atlas

Nationalities and languages also begin with a capital letter.

Australian	German
Indonesian	Korean
Spanish	French
Egyptian	Russian
Hindu	Japanese
South African	Chinese
British	English
Pakistani	Cantonese

You also use a capital letter for the first letter in words and phrases that you use for saying **hello** and **goodbye**.

Exercise 1

Put the correct punctuation mark at the end of each sentence.

1. Sally is my sister's friend

2. What time is it

3. Don't speak to your mother like that

4. Good morning Did you sleep well

5. Oh dear Did he hurt himself

6. Mom asked if I had cleaned my room

7. Help I'm falling

8. Could you open a window, please

9. He's very handsome, isn't he

10. What a lovely day

Exercise 2

Rewrite the following sentences by putting commas and apostrophes in the correct places.

1. This food is delicious isnt it?

   _____

2. Hello David. Have you seen Toms new bike?

   _____

3. "Good morning children" said Miss Lee.

   _____

4. I cant speak French very well.

   _____

5. Excuse me Mr. Chen. Could you help me with this question please.

   _____

6. Sams mom bought rice eggs and flour.

   _____

7. Yes thank you. Ive had a lovely day.

   _____

8. Shes my big brothers girlfriend.

   _____

Put capital letters in the correct places as you rewrite these sentences.

1. have you seen mr. chen?

   _____

2. can I help with the cooking, mom?

   _____

3. we went to paris for a holiday.

   _____

4. "do you like my new car?" asked uncle david.

   _____

5. we visited new york and saw the statue of liberty.

   _____

6. my friend doesn't speak english.

   _____

7. they spent christmas in london.

   _____

8. we went to the library on thursday.

   _____

9. were you born in june or july?

   _____

10. have you read *the lord of the rings* by j.r.r. tolkien?

    _____

11. they're going to italy next summer.

    _____

12. have a good day, mrs. park.

    _____

A List of Irregular Verbs

Here is a table to remind you of the forms of irregular verbs.

Simple Present	Third Person Singular	Present Participle	Simple Past	Past Participle
be	am, is, are	being	was	been
beat	beats	beating	beat	beaten
become	becomes	becoming	became	become
begin	begins	beginning	began	begun
bend	bends	bending	bent	bent
bite	bites	biting	bit	bitten
blow	blows	blowing	blew	blown
break	breaks	breaking	broke	broken
bring	brings	bringing	brought	brought
build	builds	building	built	built
burn	burns	burning	burned	burned
burst	bursts	bursting	burst	burst
buy	buys	buying	bought	bought
catch	catches	catching	caught	caught
choose	chooses	choosing	chose	chosen
come	comes	coming	came	come
creep	creeps	creeping	crept	crept
cut	cuts	cutting	cut	cut
dig	digs	digging	dug	dug
do	does	doing	did	done
draw	draws	drawing	drew	drawn

Simple Present	Third Person Singular	Present Participle	Simple Past	Past Participle
drink	drinks	drinking	drank	drunk
drive	drives	driving	drove	driven
eat	eats	eating	ate	eaten
fall	falls	falling	fell	fallen
feed	feeds	feeding	fed	fed
feel	feels	feeling	felt	felt
fight	fights	fighting	fought	fought
find	finds	finding	found	found
fly	flies	flying	flew	flown
forget	forgets	forgetting	forgot	forgotten
freeze	freezes	freezing	froze	frozen
get	gets	getting	got	got
give	gives	giving	gave	given
go	goes	going	went	gone
grow	grows	growing	grew	grown
have	has	having	had	had
hear	hears	hearing	heard	heard
hide	hides	hiding	hid	hidden
hit	hits	hitting	hit	hit
hold	holds	holding	held	held
hurt	hurts	hurting	hurt	hurt
keep	keeps	keeping	kept	kept
kneel	kneels	kneeling	knelt	knelt
know	knows	knowing	knew	known
lay	lays	laying	laid	laid
lead	leads	leading	led	led

Simple Present	Third Person Singular	Present Participle	Simple Past	Past Participle
learn	learns	learning	learned	learned
leave	leaves	leaving	left	left
lend	lends	lending	lent	lent
let	lets	letting	let	let
lie	lies	lying	lay	lain
light	lights	lighting	lit/lighted	lit/lighted
lose	loses	losing	lost	lost
make	makes	making	made	made
meet	meets	meeting	met	met
pay	pays	paying	paid	paid
put	puts	putting	put	put
read	reads	reading	read	read
ride	rides	riding	rode	ridden
ring	rings	ringing	rang	rung
rise	rises	rising	rose	risen
run	runs	running	ran	run
say	says	saying	said	said
see	sees	seeing	saw	seen
sell	sells	selling	sold	sold
send	sends	sending	sent	sent
shake	shakes	shaking	shook	shaken
shine	shines	shining	shone	shone
shoot	shoots	shooting	shot	shot
show	shows	showing	showed	shown
shut	shuts	shutting	shut	shut
sing	sings	singing	sang	sung

Simple Present	Third Person Singular	Present Participle	Simple Past	Past Participle
sink	sinks	sinking	sank	sunk
sit	sits	sitting	sat	sat
sleep	sleeps	sleeping	slept	slept
smell	smells	smelling	smelled	smelled
speak	speaks	speaking	spoke	spoken
spend	spends	spending	spent	spent
spread	spreads	spreading	spread	spread
steal	steals	stealing	stole	stolen
stick	sticks	sticking	stuck	stuck
sweep	sweeps	sweeping	swept	swept
swell	swells	swelling	swelled	swollen
swim	swims	swimming	swam	swum
swing	swings	swinging	swung	swung
take	takes	taking	took	taken
teach	teaches	teaching	taught	taught
tear	tears	tearing	tore	torn
tell	tells	telling	told	told
think	thinks	thinking	thought	thought
throw	throws	throwing	threw	thrown
understand	understands	understanding	understood	understood
wake	wakes	waking	woke	woken
wear	wears	wearing	wore	worn
weep	weeps	weeping	wept	wept
win	wins	winning	won	won
write	writes	writing	wrote	written